D1057933

The
Lenten
Tree

Devotions
for Children and Adults
To prepare for
CHRIST'S DEATH
and
HIS RESURRECTION

Dean Meador Smith

Illustrations by Ginger Meador

Abingdon Press
Nashville

The Lenten Tree

Published by Abingdon Press 2004
Copyright © 2001 by Dean Meador Smith
All rights reserved

Original printing, September 2001
Designed by Cynthia Clark

No part of this work may be reproduced or transmitted in any form or by any means, electronic or mechanical, including photocopying and recording or by any information storage or retrieval system, except as may be expressly permitted by the 1976 Copyright Act or by permission in writing from the publisher.
Requests for permission should be submitted in writing to:
Abingdon Press, P. O. Box 801, 201 Eighth Avenue South, Nashville, Tennessee 37202-0801; faxed to (615)749-6128; or sent via e-mail to permission@abingdonpress.com.

Scripture quotations marked (NIV) are taken from the HOLY BIBLE, NEW INTERNATIONAL VERSION®. Copyright © 1973, 1978, 1984 by International Bible Society. Used by permission of Zondervan Publishing House. All rights reserved.

Scripture quotations marked (TLB) are taken from *The Living Bible*, copyright © 1971. Used by permission of Tyndale House Publishers, Inc., Wheaton, IL 60189. All rights reserved.

Scripture quotations marked (KJV) are taken from the King James or Authorized Version of the Bible.

Dag Hammarskjold quote from *Markings*, translated by Leif Sjoberg and W. H. Auden. Copyright © 1964 by Alfred A. Knopf Inc., and Faber and Faber, Ltd. Reprinted by permission of Random House, Inc.

Prayer from *The Prayers of Peter Marshall* edited by Catherine Marshall, copyright © 1954 by Catherine Marshall. Used by permission of Baker Book House.

ISBN 0-687-06279-9

04 05 06 07 08 09 10 11 12 13–10 9 8 7 6 5 4 3 2 1

MANUFACTURED IN THE UNITED STATES OF AMERICA

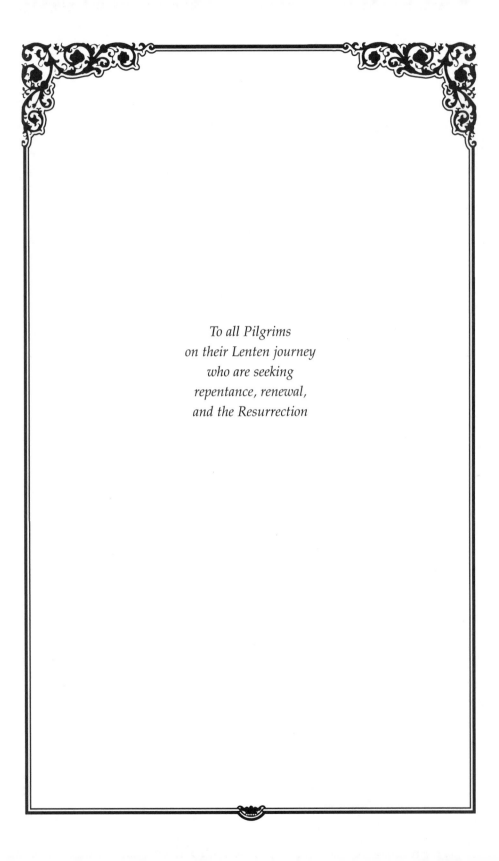

*To all Pilgrims
on their Lenten journey
who are seeking
repentance, renewal,
and the Resurrection*

A note to Parents

Some of the concepts presented in this book will be too complex or intense for younger children. Please read the day's selection <u>in advance</u> and adapt for the ages of your children. As the parent, you will best know the comprehension level of your children.

Contents

Preface

Many years ago during my college years, I spent the summer traveling through Europe. One of my most vivid memories is standing in "a waiting room" of some Christian catacombs. This room was where the first century followers of Christ stood to hear the gospel message. These young converts were not allowed into the assembly room of the baptized believers until they had gone through forty days of rigorous training in the Christian faith.

I remember imagining myself as one of these early followers and thinking how they went against the grain of their culture and their society to become a follower of Christ. During this special time of preparation for baptism, the converts received careful instruction of the Christian creed. They examined their lives: their misplaced loyalties, their sins, and their need for Christ. They constantly fasted, confessed their sins, and prayed for transformation and revelation. On the Saturday evening before Easter, a service was held, and the believers were baptized. The following day, Easter Sunday, they were able to join the assembly to pray and celebrate Christ's resurrection. I remember feeling how they must have eagerly anticipated receiving the Lord's Supper with the body of believers, His church. The young converts had gone through a time of waiting, weeping, and learning how to live in Christ. They had weighed the cost of being a Christian and chosen to follow in the steps of Jesus.

This is what Lent is about. It is the forty days before Easter (not counting Sundays), beginning with Ash Wednesday and ending the night before Easter. It is a time of silence and waiting—a time of revelation, conversion, and transformation. Lent is a time of remembering. It is a time to pause, retreat from our busy life, and to reflect on what Christ has done and wants to do in our lives. It is a time Christ is revealed to us through the symbols and stories in God's Word. It is a time to encounter Christ and His journey through life. We hear His teachings, see His example, and follow Him to the cross. We remember the Passion of our Lord and how He gave His life so that we may live. We remember and whisper, "For me He died."

Lent is a time of giving up areas in our life for spiritual discipline. These negative ways may be fears that paralyze us, worries that never happen, or sins that separate us from our loving Christ. Lent is a time of transformation. It is a time for taking up something that will bear the fruits of our being "born again." Through prayer and meditation, we become the persons God created us to be. We become forgiven pilgrims "made over" to walk in His Steps.

Lent is a time to look for the Easter Sunrise and celebrate Christ's victory over death. In my book *The Advent Jesse Tree,* my prayer was for you to experience the power of the Advent season as you prepared for the coming of Christ at Christmas. My prayer for this book is that it will help in preparing yourself for Easter. May God bless you during this time of repentance and renewal!

Acknowledgments

N book is written alone. I have received abundant inspiration from people who have lived the Christian faith around me. Without them knowing, they have shown me how to walk the pilgrim's journey of Lent. I have seen Christ in them through their sermons, their godly living, and their persevering through the wildernesses of life.

Words cannot express my gratitude for the illustrator of this book, Ginger Meador. Many hours were spent in prayer and in researching the symbols used for this book. The result came with Spirit inspired drawings. These illustrations stand alone in proclaiming the gospel message and will greatly impact future generations with the Salvation story.

A big thank you goes to Bonnie McGee, my forever friend. She not only proofed the devotions and made suggestions on improvements but also provided the constant affirmation to see that this book was completed. Her prayer has always been that this book would lead to Christ and the bearing of His fruit.

I am very grateful to Cynthia Clark of Quail Ridge Press for her artistic design and untiring work in producing such a beautiful book. Also, a special thank you goes to Barney McKee, a most endearing and talented man. Without his support, this book would never have come together.

This book has taken me ten years to write, and Elizabeth, Emily, and Erin, my three daughters, have cheered me every step of the way. They have put up with hours of typing and many nights without supper to see this book brought to fruition. They knew their mother felt a calling from God, and they supported that calling all the way.

Finally, I thank my husband, Eddie, for being my soul mate in this endeavor. He is my greatest encourager and has always been there to help me think through a thought or show me other routes I might take with the messages in this book.

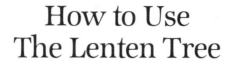

How to Use
The Lenten Tree

The Lenten Tree book is designed for use during the 40 days of Lent. The devotions will begin on Ash Wednesday and continue each day (excluding Sundays) until the Saturday night before Easter morning. There is also a 41st devotion to celebrate the Resurrection of our Lord on Easter Sunday.

The devotions center around symbols which represent areas of Jesus Christ and His life:

- **Who Jesus Christ is:** a baby child, a seed, the living water, the bread of life, the tabernacle, a rock, a priest, a goat, the vine with branches, the lily of the valleys, a robe and crown, and the bread and wine
- **His ministry on earth:** The stones in the wilderness, the dove, a fish, the wedding miracle, a boat, a lamp, and the healing of the paralytic man
- **The foretelling of His blood sacrifice:** fig leaves, a lamb, the hyssop, the Ark of Covenant, a bronze snake, the veil, a cross
- **The events leading up to His death and resurrection:** a big fish, a bottle of perfume, praying hands, a rooster, 30 pieces of silver, a flagellum, a crown of thorns, a donkey, palm branches, a nail, a spear, a wash basin and towel, the chrysalis with butterfly, and an empty egg

Each symbol is explained with scriptures, devotions, questions, prayers, a memory verse, and songs. Use the symbols and devotions for your Lenten meditations or quiet time. There are also some Lenten activities to do with your family. Children learn by doing, and these activities will make the lessons they learn during Lent more meaningful.

The illustrations in this book beautifully portray the symbols and may be used to make ornaments for a small tree. Permission is given to copy these illustrations to hang on the tree. You may choose to make or buy your ornaments.

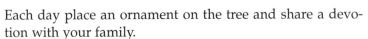

Each day place an ornament on the tree and share a devotion with your family.

Lent is a time that children can learn how much Jesus loves them and the great sacrifice He made for their eternal life. This book is designed to introduce and bring them to Jesus. It then shows them how Jesus lived and the example they are to follow as Christians. The adult devotions are intended for realization, reflection, and resolve to walk in His steps.

Symbols

Day 1.   ashes making a cross
Day 2.   stones in the wilderness
Day 3.   fig leaves
Day 4.   a baby child
Day 5.   a seed
Day 6.   a lamb
Day 7.   a hyssop branch
Day 8.   the Ark of Covenant
Day 9.   water (the living water)
Day 10. manna (the bread of life)
Day 11. a bronze snake and pole
Day 12. the veil
Day 13. the tabernacle
Day 14. a rock
Day 15. a priest
Day 16. a big fish
Day 17. a goat
Day 18. a dove
Day 19. a fish
Day 20. a jar of water (the first miracle)
Day 21. a boat
Day 22. a vine with branches
Day 23. a lamp (five foolish and five wise women)
Day 24. a mat for the paralytic man
Day 25. a lily
Day 26. a bottle of perfume
Day 27. praying hands
Day 28. a rooster
Day 29. thirty pieces of silver
Day 30. a flagellum or whip
Day 31. a crown of thorns
Day 32. a robe and crown
Day 33. a donkey

Day 34. palm branches (Palm Sunday)

Day 35. a nail

Day 36. a spear

Day 37. a wash basin and towel

Day 38. the bread and cup (Maundy Thursday)

Day 39. the cross (Good Friday)

Day 40. a chrysalis with a butterfly emerging

Day 41. an empty Easter egg (Easter Sunday)

The Journey's Beginning

Symbol: ashes making a cross

Memory Verse: "Create in me a clean heart, O God; and renew a right spirit within me." Psalm 51:10 (KJV)

Songs to Sing:
   "Lord, I Want to Be a Christian"
   "I Surrender All"
   "Just As I Am"

The Journey's Beginning
(CHILDREN)

Scriptures: Psalm 51:1-2

Devotion: Is there a messy closet in your house? If there is, then you might need to help your family with some spring-cleaning. This is a time to take out any old clothes or toys that you don't use and put everything else in order. You will have to work very hard sweeping out dusty old cobwebs or deciding what to throw away, but when you finish, your room will be very neat and clean, and it will make you feel good!

Do you remember a man named David in the Bible? There was a time when he wanted to do some cleaning. It was not in his house, however. It was in his heart. He was very sorry for something he had done, so he prayed to God and asked God to take all the bad out of his life. He asked God to wash him and make him clean. God knew David was sorry for what he had done, so He forgave him and cleaned up the dirty closet in David's heart.

Are you sorry for something you have done or said? You can't clean your heart, but God can. He gave us the Bible to show us how He would do it. He would send His only Son, Jesus, to die on a cross so that we would be clean from all our sins. This is hard to understand, so God gave us symbols in the Bible to help us. For the next few weeks, we are going to take a journey, a journey to the cross. By looking at these symbols and God's Word, we will see what Jesus did for us and how He calls us to follow Him. Are you ready to get started?

(Show symbol) Ashes had great meaning to God's people in the Bible. They would put ashes on themselves to show they were very sad or sorry about something. Some would place ashes on their faces or even sit in them! Ashes help remind us that we need to be sorry for our sin, just like David was. Then we can turn to God, and He will make us new and clean inside.

Questions:
   Why did David want God to clean his heart?
   What do ashes remind us of?
   Are you sorry for your sin?

Prayer: Dear God, I am very sorry for _____. Please forgive me of this. I want to stop sinning, and I want to be very clean for you. Teach me Your way and help me follow You. Amen.

A Lenten Activity: On Ash Wednesday, many Christians place the sign of the cross on their foreheads with ashes to symbolize that they belong to Christ and that they are sorry for their sins. This act could help your child begin his or her journey to the cross.

The Journey's Beginning
(ADULTS)

Scriptures: Leviticus 19:1-2, 17-18; Psalm 51; Isaiah 22:12-13; Ephesians 4:22-24

Devotion: "Eat, drink, and be merry, for tomorrow we die" (Isaiah 22:13) has become, for many, the slogan of life. During Mardi Gras, it can be reinterpreted as, "Party hard, for tomorrow is Lent." The day after Fat Tuesday in New Orleans, a television news station reported that the city measures how successful the season has been by the amount of trash left in the streets. The more excess, the better. Garbage workers are seen knee high in debris on the streets cleaning up. Another successful year in the life of our culture.

   During Lent, however, we are called to a journey of counterculture. Instead of feasts and self-indulgence, there is fasting and the giving up of negative ways. Instead of excess, there is a change to introspection and simple living. Instead of "doing what feels good," there is the command to "Be holy" (Lev. 19:1-2) even if it brings rejection and pain. Instead of "living for the day," we are to remember our mortality— "We are dust, and unto dust we shall return."

Lent is also a time of "putting on." This is when we add disciplines to our life such as devotional or prayer time to bring us closer to Christ. These deeds help us remember the Passion of our Lord and the love He showed for us in giving His life so that we may live.

The people, in Isaiah 22, had given up hope. Lent is a season for regaining faith and joy in the goodness of God's power. Psalm 51 was written by a man who had to face who he was and what terrible deed he had done. He could have stayed in the ash heap of shame and disillusionment, but his broken and contrite heart, a whole heart turning to God, was lifted by the grace of forgiveness, the cleansing of his spirit, and the joyful singing of God's righteousness.

Are you willing to allow God to change you, to take on God's values instead of the world's values? Are you willing to give humbly to God and others, depriving yourself of status, prestige, wealth, and security? Are you willing to leave everything behind you to walk in the footsteps of Christ? If so, begin this pilgrimage of Lent leading to Easter. God will resurrect us from our dust and ashes, make us new creatures, and bring us life out of death. Expect a miracle to happen.

Prayer: Psalm 51

DAY TWO

Jesus in the Wilderness

Symbol: stones

Memory Verse: "Man shall not live by bread alone, but by every word that proceedeth out of the mouth of God." Matthew 4:4 (KJV)

Songs to Sing:
   "Take Time to Be Holy"
   "Be Still My Soul"
   "I Want Jesus to Walk with Me"

Jesus in the Wilderness
(CHILDREN)

Scriptures: Matthew 4:1-11

Devotion: Do you know what temptation is? Temptation makes you want to do something that you know is wrong. Maybe you are very hungry and you see cookies in a cookie jar. You know it's just before dinner, and you're not supposed to eat sweets. There's a little voice inside you that tells you no one will know if you just take one cookie. We call this *temptation*. Did you know Jesus was tempted in the same way? Let's read our scripture.( )

Jesus was very hungry. He had not eaten breakfast, lunch, or dinner. In fact, He had not eaten for 40 days! The devil, God's enemy, came to Jesus and told Him to turn some stones into bread. But Jesus would not listen to the devil. Even though He was hungry, He knew He would be doing what the devil wanted instead of what God wanted. Jesus only does what God says, and so He told the devil to get away from Him and to not tempt Him anymore.

The devil kept trying to get Jesus to disobey God. He told Jesus he would give Him a lot of things if Jesus would just worship him. But Jesus said "No!" every time. Jesus loved God, His Father. He never did anything wrong, and He obeyed God every day. He even obeyed Him by going to the cross to die for us.

Now, if we love Jesus, we will try to do what He wants us to do. Sometimes it may be hard to be good, and we will be tempted, but Jesus will never leave us. Angels helped Jesus, and He will help us if we turn to Him. Just say "No!" to the tempter, and "Yes!" to God.

Questions:
Why was Jesus hungry?
Who tried to get Jesus to do something wrong?
What did Jesus do?

Prayer: Dear Jesus, thank you for doing what God wanted

You to do instead of what the devil wanted. Help us to obey God and to say "No!" whenever the devil wants us to do wrong.

A Lenten Activity: Make hot cross buns to eat (see Appendix). They look like stones but can show how Christ obeyed God by choosing the cross. Legend has it that two days before Easter, a monk saw some poor hungry families living in ragged tents on the streets of England. Engraving a cross on the top of baked rolls, he went out and fed the families physically and then spiritually by sharing the Easter story. Thus, the tradition of eating hot cross buns during the Lenten season was born.

Jesus in the Wilderness
(ADULTS)

Scriptures: Matthew 4:1-11; I Corinthians 10:12-13; II Timothy 3:1-6; Hebrews 2:18, 4:15; James 1:2-4

Devotion: The journey of life is sometimes like a roller coaster ride with highs followed by immediate lows. So it was with Jesus as He was led into the wilderness after His baptism. Hearing that He was the beloved Son with whom God was pleased, it would have been easy for Jesus to stay on top. Everyone would know His name. Opportunities to do good for others would be available because He would be all-powerful in an earthly kingdom. Instead, Jesus chose to journey into the wilderness to experience silence, waiting, and temptation—lots of temptation. The devil would offer shortcuts to glory. Jesus would choose to listen to God's voice and follow the long and painful way to the cross.

Many resist the wilderness because it conjures up images of aimless wandering, hardship, and loneliness. If they do enter, the obstacles may seem insurmountable with no way out. Faith wavers and depression sets in. With the very existence of life threatened, there is no strength to grow "character." The wilderness, however, can be a place of revelation instead of aimless wandering. Even though it is painful, we can experience our own inadequacy and the need for something more than just "bread." This awareness can transform our lives into total dependence on God through Christ. Intimacy is gained with the One who understands all our temptations and hurts. We are sustained and guided by Him, the Way through our wilderness.

It was once said that when God was creating the earth, He dropped a few stones in the Rocky Mountains. When He got to Israel, the bag broke! The wilderness of Israel is full of stones. It is comforting to know that the stones of temptation were everywhere, yet Christ conquered the wilderness. The devil's aim was to bring Him to sin against God. In doing this, he would render Christ incapable forever of being the Sacrifice for the sins of others. Being tempted in all things, however, Christ never fell to temptation, thus overcoming the tempter. The adversary and his demons are great, but Christ is greater. May we gain strength from this victory, obeying God when the demon voices of self-pity, revenge, and hopelessness are heard.

Prayer: God of wisdom, accompany us through the perilous journeys of whatever wilderness awaits us. On our road to Easter, give us a spirit of discernment among the voices we hear. As He went before us to show us Your way, may we be bold to follow His example. Amen.

The First Sacrifice

Symbol: fig leaves

Memory Verse: "Your life is now hidden with Christ in God." Colossians 3:3 (NIV)

Songs to Sing:
  "Calvary Covers It All"
  "Are You Washed in the Blood?"
  "Jesus Paid It All"

The First Sacrifice
(CHILDREN)

Scriptures: Genesis 3:1-21; Colossians 3:3

Devotion: Do you remember the story of Adam and Eve? Their best friend was God, and they would walk and talk with Him in a beautiful garden that He had created for them. God let them do anything they wanted except for one thing. Do you know what that one thing was? God told them the tree in the middle of the garden was not to be touched, and the fruit was not to be eaten. If they did this, they would die. Along came a snake, who really was the devil. The snake told Eve that God was wrong, and Eve listened to the devil's words. She and Adam both ate the fruit. They realized they had disobeyed God, and something did die inside them. Sin came in. It spoiled a beautiful friendship, and that was worse than dying! They were so ashamed that they made clothes out of fig leaves. They tried to hide from God because they didn't want Him to know they had done wrong.

But God sees everything, doesn't He? He even knows what you are thinking. He told Adam and Eve they would have to leave the beautiful garden, and they would have to work hard for food. This was a very sad time, and God knew that it would not be perfect outside the garden. He loved them and wanted to protect them from the rain and the cold. The clothes of fig leaves wouldn't be enough, so He killed an animal that He had created and made warm clothes out of the skins. Even though Adam and Eve had made Him very sad, He was willing to provide a way to save them.

Today when we do wrong, God provides a way for us to be saved. If we say we are sorry, He will forgive us. We can be new people again because God's son, Jesus, was willing to die for us on the cross.

Questions:
  Can you hide from God?
  What are some things you've done wrong that you've
    tried to hide?
  What happened to Adam and Eve when they disobeyed
    God?
  What did God do for them?

Prayer: We thank You that You still love us and are willing
to provide a way to take care of us if we are sorry for our sin.
Clothe us with Jesus Christ and help us to obey. Amen.

The First Sacrifice
(ADULTS)

Scriptures: Genesis 3:1-21; Isaiah 61:10; Romans 13:12-14;
I Corinthians 15:52-57; Galatians 3:26-27; Colossians 3:1-21

Devotion: Most of us will admit that we are not perfect
beings. Not a day goes by that an unloving deed is committed or an unkind thought passes through each of our minds.
These unloving deeds and unkind thoughts remind us that
indeed we are sinful beings and have allowed the devil to
tempt us to live in our wills instead of God's will. We try to
hide our wrongs from God by covering them up with more
sins. Also, as in the case of most guilt ridden people, we
frantically do as many good deeds as we can, hoping God
will be pleased with them and won't notice the dark condition of our heart.

Our ancestors, Adam and Eve, showed us that no matter
how many fig leaves are sewn together, sin still remains
(Genesis 3:7). The only way to be rid of sin and clothed in
righteousness is through a sacrifice by God, not man. In
Genesis 3:21, the first shedding of blood occurs, a loving act
of a Father to cover the sins of His children. This act fore-

shadows the ultimate sacrifice required for sins to be forgiven—the shedding of the blood of Jesus Christ. Take comfort in the truth that it is God, not man with his fig leaves, who will perfect us with salvation.

Prayer: Dear God, there are so many things we have done wrong in our lives, and we are so ashamed. We have been trying to hide our wrongs so no one will know, but we realize that we cannot deal with our guilt alone. In order to forgive ourselves, we must have forgiveness from the One we have offended. We are unworthy to ask Your forgiveness. We need a Savior. We turn to the cross for our salvation. Amen.

DAY FOUR

God Among Us

Symbol: a baby child

Memory Verse: "And the Word was made flesh and dwelt among us." John 1:14 (KJV)

Songs to Sing:
   "Let All Mortal Flesh Keep Silence"
   "Redeeming Love"
   "O Little Town of Bethlehem"

Thought for the Day: "For him who looks toward the future, the manger is situated on Golgotha, and the cross has already been raised in Bethlehem." Dag Hammarskjold

God Among Us
(CHILDREN)

Scriptures: Luke 2:7,21,25-38; Galatians 4:4-5

Devotion: Do you remember Adam and Eve and how they disobeyed God? This made Him very sad, and He made them leave the beautiful garden He had made for them. What do your parents do when you do something wrong? They do this because they love you and want you to do right. God knew that there needed to be punishment for Adam and Eve's sin and for all of our sin, but He loved us and wanted to save us from that punishment. He needed to find someone who would be willing to take our punishment. Then there would be no more sickness or sadness, and we could be with Him.

Do you remember how Jesus came into the world as a baby? Do you know what we call that day? (Christmas) Jesus lived in heaven with God long before that first Christmas. Yet, He was willing to leave heaven and come down to earth as a little baby. Even though He had done nothing wrong, He knew that one day, He would have to die on a cross, so we could be saved from our sin. When He was eight days old, His parents took him to church, and there they met a good man named Simeon. Simeon had been waiting to see God's baby Son. He took the child in his arms and held him very close because he knew that this was the child who would save us. Joseph named the child "Jesus," which means Savior. He knew that Jesus would take care of God's people, and that made His parents very happy!

What a change it was for Jesus to come down from heaven to earth. There is no sickness in Heaven, no sadness or sin. And yet, Jesus was willing to leave His beautiful home, to become a little baby for us. He was willing to hurt and cry, just like we do when we are sad. Jesus lived on earth for thirty-three years. He was very good and kind just like God is. He healed the sick and made the blind see. He was even willing to die for us.

Questions:
Where was Jesus before He was born?
Why was Simeon so happy?
How did Jesus show us that God is good and kind?

Prayer: Jesus, thank You for loving us so much that you were willing to come from heaven to earth to be a baby. Thank you for showing us how good and kind Your Father is by your life. And most important of all, thank you for being willing to die for us, so we would not have to be punished for our sins. Jesus, You are our Savior, and we love you. Amen.

A Lenten Activity: Make cinnamon rolls and place a plastic baby (Jesus, our King) in them (see Appendix).

God Among Us
(ADULTS)

Scriptures: Luke 2:21-39; John 1:10-14; Galatians 4:4-5; Philippians 2:1-16; Hebrews 2:9,14-15

Devotion: Today we learn a lesson on humility. The incarnation was the act of the preexistent Son of God voluntarily assuming a human body and human nature. Without ceasing to be God, He willingly emptied Himself to place, time, and other human limitations. Residing in our world, He had no earthly riches but suffered the same pains all of us as sinful humans encounter. He put Himself in our place.

Because Jesus was born of a woman, He was human. He was subject to the laws God had given Moses. Failure to obey the laws resulted in death unless a perfect unblemished lamb gave its blood to cover the sins of the people. Thus Jesus was the perfect sacrifice because although He was fully human, He was without sin. His death was the final sacrifice needed to bring those of us who are enslaved to sin into God's family.

Jesus voluntarily laid aside His divine rights and privileges out of love and obedience for His Father. He willingly suffered and endured pain so that He could reach out to us with compassion when we hurt. The lowest step of humiliation was when He died on the cross, suffering not only physical pain but the public ridicule of a slave's death. For Jesus was not only God's servant, but also man's as well.

If it is difficult for us to identify with Christ's servant attitude, perhaps we need to evaluate our own motives. Are we more interested in power or service, getting or giving? Christ gave us the example of putting others first. We can approach life expecting to be served, or we can look for opportunities to serve others. Christ being born human shows us what we are to become—true servants to others.

Prayer: Jesus, we bow before You at Your name. We are humbled to think how You would leave the glories of Heaven to become our Servant. You have become a Light unto the world to show us how to live. Rearrange our attitudes, desires, and motives, and give us the power to live as sensitive servants, reaching out to others who hurt.

The Seed

Gmeador

Symbol: a seed

Memory Verse: "I am the resurrection, and the life: he that believeth in me, though he were dead, yet shall he live: And whosoever liveth and believeth in me shall never die." John 11:25-26 (KJV)

Songs to Sing:
   "Soon and Very Soon"
   "Hymn of Promise"
   "Now the Green Blade Riseth"

The Seed
(CHILDREN)

Scriptures: Genesis 22:18; John 11:25-26, 12:23-24; I Corinthians 15:36

Devotion: Do you remember how Jesus was willing to come down from heaven to become a little baby? He lived for 33 years, and then it was time for Him to go back to heaven. Do you know how he would be able to do that? He told us to look in our gardens and to find a seed for the answer.

Do you know what happens to a seed when you plant it in the ground? It sleeps for awhile, and then it begins to fall apart and die. Soon something amazing happens. Water begins to give it food, and along with the soil, it helps the dead seed start to grow again. When the green leaf comes out of the ground, it looks very different from the seed that is first planted. It is a miracle!

A long time ago, God told a man named Abraham that a Seed would come, and Abraham believed Him.

This Seed is Jesus Christ, and He would save all people who do wrong if they are truly sorry. All they would have to do is just believe in the Seed. It was wonderful for God to do this for us, wasn't it? The Seed would have to do something, though. He would have to die, and then He would be able to gather all His children in His arms to protect them.

Jesus was willing to do this for us, and so a long time ago He died on a cross. They put Him in a tomb, and it looked like He was dead. But He was only waiting, just like a seed, to shoot forth out of the tomb into the light. The Bible says when you plant a seed, it cannot grow unless it dies first. Jesus could not go back to heaven until He died first. He was willing to do that for us. He must love us very much!

Questions:
How does a flower grow?
Who is our Seed?
What did Jesus have to do for us?

Prayer: Jesus, it is hard to believe You were willing to die for us, and yet You did. Every time we see a flower, help us remember a seed had to die for that flower to live. Help us to trust in Your Seed, Jesus Christ. Amen.

A Lenten Activity: Plant some seeds today. It could be daffodils, lilies, or even dandelions. Watch them grow, and during your Lenten journey, remember the miracle of the Easter Seed!

The Seed
(ADULTS)

Scriptures: Genesis 22:18; I Corinthians 15:29-58; John 2:19-22, 11:25, 26, 12:23-28; Galatians 3:8-19

Devotion: In the Bible God in His grace had made a covenant with Abraham about the Seed that would bless the entire world. Righteousness would come by faith in this Seed and not by the law that Moses would later introduce.

Christ foretold the return to His glory in heaven via the ultimate humiliation—His death. He would have to fall to the earth and die in order to produce salvation for many souls—a plentiful harvest of new life. He would lay in the earth like seed, only to come up again green and flourishing.

When a seed is placed in the earth, it undergoes a time of dormancy, activity being suspended. Like our organic bodies, decomposition begins to occur. The seed's cover is chemically broken down, allowing water to enter. The weakening of the cover begins another process called germination in which the plant embryo within the seed resumes growth. The green shoot that comes out of the ground looks very different from the seed first planted.

Paul explained the difference in our newly resurrected bodies so beautifully in I Corinthians 15. Our original Adam bodies are made from the earth, but all who become Christ's will one day have His body—a body from heaven. Death is swallowed up in victory through the dying of this Seed, Jesus Christ our Lord! We cannot understand it, but we only have to look at the miracle of a seed to realize it can happen!

During this Lenten season, Jesus asks us to become like a seed, dying to our love of the things of this world. We must become weak to our self-will and allow the fertile soil of grace and the One who is beyond time to grow us into flourishing flowers, offering refreshment to the heavy laden. The exchange for our death to the world is priceless—it is eternal glory!

Prayer: We are so much in love with the life of the world. Help us to realize that the things of this world are vain and insufficient to make us truly happy. Open our eyes to anything that is causing us to not put You first, and make it so despicable that we will turn from it. Thank you for your promise that even though death will come to everyone, eternal life will be ours if we believe in You.

The Passover Lamb

Symbol: a lamb

Memory Verses: "When I see the blood, I will pass over you." Exodus 12:13 (KJV)

"For Christ, our Passover lamb, has been sacrificed."
I Corinthians 5:7 (NIV)

Songs to Sing:
 "Worthy Is the Lamb That Was Slain"
 "Only Trust Him"
 "Just As I Am"

The Passover Lamb
(CHILDREN)

Scriptures: Exodus 12:3-7, 12-13; I Corinthians 5:7; I Peter 1:19

Devotion: A long time ago, the people of Israel had become slaves to the people of Egypt. They had to work hard and had very little food. God did not want His people to be slaves, but the king of Egypt would not let them go.

So God sent ten bad things to happen to the land of Egypt. The last thing was that God would kill all the first born children. He had a plan, however, to save all who trusted in Him. He told the people to take the blood of a perfect lamb and to put it on the sides and the top of the doors of their houses. If a family obeyed God and marked the door of their house with the blood of the lamb, He would pass over the house, and no children would be killed. That night, the Lord killed all the firstborn children in Egypt, including the king's son. The king got up during the night and saw his son was dead. But no one was dead in the houses where the blood had been sprinkled on the sides and tops of the doors. The king was very sad, so he told the children of Israel to leave Egypt. They would no more be slaves. Today, this holiday is called Passover, and it is still celebrated by many people all over the world.

If God told you to do this to your house, would you do it? I'm sure the children of Israel wondered how the blood of a little lamb on their door could save them from death. They chose to believe, however, and because of their simple faith, they were freed. When Jesus died on the cross, He shed His blood for you so that you might be free. You might not fully understand what this means, but if you believe it and trust in Jesus, then you will be saved, just like the children of Israel. Do you believe in Jesus?

Questions:
What were the people told to put on the sides and over
their door?
Why did they do this?
Did the king put the blood on the door of his house?

Prayer: Jesus, thank You for being my Lamb. Thank You for
dying for me and for passing over my sins. I love You.
Amen.

A Lenten Activity: Celebrate the Passover meal, or Seder,
with your family as a reminder that we are all God's chosen
people if we believe in Jesus (see Appendix). Make it a time
of thanking Christ for becoming the final "Lamb," sacrificed
in order that our joy may be full.

The Passover Lamb
(ADULTS)

Scriptures: Exodus 12:1-13; I Corinthians 5:7; Hebrews 2:14-
15; I Peter 1:19

Devotion: The Passover feast was established to celebrate
Israel's deliverance from Egypt and to remind the people of
how God had delivered them from the plagues and slavery.
From this point on in history, the Hebrew people would
clearly understand that for them to be spared from death, an
innocent life had to be sacrificed in their place. The unblemished lamb, now called the Paschal lamb, is a type of the
true Lamb, Jesus Christ. The Crucifixion story, showing the
justice of God's passing over and sparing those who are
sprinkled with the blood of Christ, parallels the Passover.
The Passover was observed in the month of Abib, which
corresponds to late March and early April on our calendar.
A year old male lamb without blemish was selected and

killed at dusk. Christ, perfect and without sin, died in the late afternoon hours (Luke 23:44-45). Caution was made to not break the bones of the lamb. So it was with Christ's body (John 19:31-37). The Passover occurred before the law was established in the Old Testament showing that it was the blood of the lamb that delivered mankind out of bondage, not the law. The lamb was a sacrifice, a substitute for the person who would have died in the plague. Christ is our substitute over the penalty of death. The lamb's death signified freedom to Israel. Christ's death redeems us.

At the Passover, it was not enough that the blood of the lamb was shed. It had to be applied to the door by the believer. The blood was to be sprinkled with a hyssop branch upon the sides and top of the door as an outwardly sign of accepting the blood's atonement. The hyssop represents faith in accepting the promise of God's protection. When we profess our faith in the blood of Christ, we will openly do our best to live and love for Him.

Prayer: Jesus, we ask You to become our personal Savior. We know that sin dwells deep within us. We know that we cannot escape from our sin on our own; only You can free us. You have shed Your blood; now it is up to us to apply that blood to our hearts. Free us from bondage, and lead us into life eternal. Amen.

The Hyssop Branch

Symbol: a hyssop branch

Memory Verse: "For the wages of sin is death, but the gift of God is eternal life through Jesus Christ our Lord." Romans 6:23 (KJV)

Songs to Sing:
  "Into My Heart"
  "I Surrender All"
  "Just As I Am"

The Hyssop Branch
(CHILDREN)

Scriptures: Exodus 12:22, 27-28; John 3:16, 19:28-30; Romans 6:23

Devotion: Do you like presents? It's fun to get them because we know whoever gave them to us must love us very much. But what if we received a present from our parents or grandparents and decided not to open it. How do you think everyone would feel? It would make the person giving the present sad because they would think you didn't want it, and it would make you feel sad because you wouldn't be able to play with the gift inside.

God had given a gift to the children of Israel and it was freedom. But the Israelites had to do something to have this gift. Let's read about it. They had to take a hyssop branch, dip it in the blood of a lamb, and put it on the sides and the top of the door to their homes. When they obeyed Him, that night God "passed over" their homes. They had received His gift and were free to follow God to a beautiful place to live.

When Jesus was on the cross, He became very thirsty. A soldier took a hyssop branch, dipped it in wine vinegar, and gave it to Jesus to drink. Jesus could have refused this gift, but instead, He drank. Then Jesus said, "It is finished," and died. He knew He had finished the job that God wanted Him to do, and that is to give a gift also, the gift of eternal life. But Jesus can't make us take the gift. We have to apply His blood to our hearts.

But how do we do this? We don't have a hyssop branch like the Israelites and the soldier had, but God has given us His Bible to show us what to do. First, we must believe that God loves us and wants us to be happy with Him. Second, we must realize we do bad things every day. This is called sin, and we need God to forgive us. Third, we must believe we are saved from our sins by the blood of Jesus on the cross. That is the gift God gives us. Finally, it's not enough to just believe these things. The devil believes this, and the devil is not a friend of God! We must take this gift and ask Jesus to come into our hearts to help us live for God. If we do this, He will come in, and we will be happy.

Questions:
   After Jesus drank from the hyssop branch, what did He say?
   What is God's gift to us?
   Have you received His gift?

Prayer: (For the nonbeliever) God, I know that I have sinned and I want to have a clean life. I ask for Jesus to come into my heart to live as my Savior. Thank You, that He has come into my life. Amen.

   (For the believer) Thank you, Father, that Jesus lives in my life. Help me to grow by praying, reading Your Word, obeying what it says, and telling others about You. Amen.

The Hyssop Branch
(ADULTS)

Scriptures: Exodus 12:22, 27-28; Psalm 51:7; John 19:28-30; Ephesians 2:8, 9; Hebrews 9:19-22

Devotion: The shedding of blood represents the Covenant, or God saving us. The hyssop branch represents faith in the Covenant for cleansing. It was not enough for the blood of a lamb to be slain at the Passover. It was what the Israelites did with the blood that counted. Not blood in a basin but blood applied on the lintel saved them from death. As the tabernacle was built and the sacrificial system established, the blood was sufficient for cleansing but not efficient unless Moses, with a hyssop branch, sprinkled it over the people and the ceremonial objects of the temple.

Throughout the Old Testament, the sprinkling of blood with the hyssop was also used to cleanse lepers or any with infectious diseases. Neither feelings nor personal worthiness could cleanse them save one thing—the blood applied with the hyssop, or faith.

In Psalm 51, David looked upon himself as a most leprous and polluted creature who needed cleansing. He asked God to purge him with hyssop. This expression alludes to the sprinkling of blood to release him from his defilement. Although he felt unworthy, David had faith in the blood. His sins were purged, and fellowship with God was restored.

We come now to the cross. Jesus taking the wine vinegar from the hyssop says, "It is finished," completing the task of which He had been called to do. He dies for the redemption of mankind. But not all the blood shed on Calvary's cross can save a soul from death unless it is applied to the heart. This simply means acknowledging Jesus Christ as the only way to bring man to God. We must then ask Christ to come and take control of our lives. With the invitation to come in, Christ takes His hyssop branch, and with His blood, cleanses us from all our unrighteousness. Then God, seeing the blood, "passes over" our sins.

The hyssop was a common weed but obtainable by everyone. It was found everywhere growing up through the rocks and out of the crevices in the walls. So it is typical of faith. Faith is available to all, and if Christ is allowed in, it can spring up in the hardest of hearts. What will you do with the blood, the blood of our Passover Lamb who died on Calvary? The decision is up to you.

Prayer: God, I acknowledge my sin and unworthiness. Only the blood of Your Son, Jesus Christ can bring me to fellowship with You. I lift up my hyssop branch to You. Cleanse me and ready me for service to others. Amen.

The Ark of Covenant

Symbol: the ark of covenant

Memory Verse: "The blood of Jesus, his Son, cleanseth us from all sin." I John 1:7 (KJV)

Songs to Sing:
   "Grace Greater Than Our Sin"
   "My Tribute"
   "Nothing but the Blood"

The Ark of Covenant
(CHILDREN)

Scriptures: Exodus 37:1-9; Leviticus 16:15-16; Hebrews 9:26-28

Devotion: Do you remember our story about Passover? God told the children of Israel to kill a lamb and cover their door with its blood. Because they did what He asked them to do, they were allowed to leave Egypt. God was going to lead His children to a very special place to live, but it would take them a long time to get there, and God knew that they would get lonely. He told Moses to make a chest so the people could know He would be with them.

Let's read about the chest. (Exodus 37:1-9)

The ark was a very special object to the people because it was their meeting place with God. They carried it everywhere they went, and they would keep it in a very special room in their church. They would even carry it into battles to show everyone that God was with them. The top of the ark was made of pure gold, and it was also very special. It was called the Atonement Cover. Do you know what atonement means? It's a big word, but all it means is "to cover" and once a year, the children of Israel would have a special Day of Atonement, a day of covering. What do you think it was that they wanted to cover? They wanted to cover their sins.

Inside the chest, Moses had placed the tablets of the Ten Commandments. These were the laws God had given the people to obey. He knew they would not always follow the laws, so He told them to kill an animal and have a priest sprinkle the blood on the cover of the chest. God promised the people that covering their sins with blood would be enough for forgiveness until a Final Sacrifice would come. Do you know who our Final Sacrifice is? Let's read Who He is (Hebrews 9:26-28).

Do you remember how God killed an animal, so He could give clothes to cover Adam and Eve? Many years later,

Christ gave His life on the cross, so our sins would be covered forever with His blood. Everyone who comes to Him will be forgiven. That's a great New Promise, isn't it?

Questions:
What was inside the chest?
What did the priest sprinkle on the top of the chest?
Why did he do this?
Who is the Final Sacrifice for us?

Prayer: God, we are so glad we don't have to kill animals to show You how sorry we are for all the bad things we do. We can't believe You loved us so much that You would send Your only Son to be the Final Sacrifice for us, but we are very glad. Help us to show love to others just as You showed love to us by covering our sins. Amen.

The Ark of Covenant
(ADULTS)

Scriptures: Exodus 24:5-8, 37:1-9; Leviticus 16:5,14-16; Psalm 51; Isaiah 53:6-7; Matthew 6:14-15; Romans 3:21-26; I Peter 1:18-21; Hebrews 9; Revelation 5:6-14, 11:19, 13:8

Devotion: Since the fall of man, the shedding of blood had been required for God's acceptance. Throughout the Old Testament, we find such events as in the covering of Adam with an animal skin, Abel bringing a sacrificial lamb, the lamb substitute for Abraham's son, and the covering of the doorposts at Passover. One of the most important places where blood was sacrificed was inside a room of the tabernacle called the Holy of Holies. There the Ark of the Covenant was kept. The chest held a copy of the law and had been created to symbolize the Old Covenant. On top of the chest was a cover called the Atonement Cover or Mercy

Seat. Once a year on the Day of Atonement, a goat was killed and its blood collected in a basin. The only way to enter the Holy of Holies was with this pure blood. The blood was then sprinkled over the Mercy Seat, signifying the covering of the sins of Israel. This was only a temporary atonement, however, and the people looked forward to the coming of the Final Sacrifice, the Lamb who would take away the sins of the world and establish the New Covenant forever.

A covenant is the closest, holiest pact that can be made with two parties. It is a solemn binding agreement. When men entered into covenant, they usually made a cut or mark in their bodies and mingled the blood. The wounds of Christ were the signs of the New Covenant ending the sacrificial system forever.

The Mercy Seat, which stands between God and the curse of the law, signifies a type of Christ. Just as God no longer saw the sins of the people because of the substitutionary atonement of the animal's blood on the seat, He now looks at the law through the blood of His Final Sacrifice, Jesus Christ.

Christ's sacrifice was not an afterthought. From the beginning of God's Word, we have seen this plan in motion. Christ Himself confirmed that the shedding of His blood is required for the forgiveness of sins. Once the plan had been completed, it would be up to us to apply His blood to our hearts. In Psalm 51, we find that God does not delight in all the sacrifices we may offer him, be it material wealth or outward deeds of service. He only desires a simple trust knowing Jesus died in our place, for our sins.

Prayer: Dear Jesus, I humbly accept You as my Final Atonement. May my sacrifice to You be a broken and contrite spirit. You alone can make me right with God. Apply Your blood to me, and empower me to live the way You taught.

DAY NINE

The Water of Life

Symbol: a spring of water

Memory Verse: "Whoever is thirsty, let him come; and whoever wishes, let him take the free gift of the water of life." Revelation 22:17 (NIV)

Songs to Sing:
   "Deep and Wide"
   "The Joy of the Lord Is My Strength"
   "Fill My Cup, Lord"
   "I've Got a River of Life"

The Water of Life
(CHILDREN)

Scripture: Exodus 15:22-27; John 4:6-14; Revelation 22:17

Devotion: The children of Israel were so hot and thirsty! For three days, they had been walking in the desert without any water to drink. There was nothing in sight except sand, rocks, and some scraggly bushes. They began to wonder why God wasn't taking care of them like He had promised. But suddenly, they saw water! Running as fast as they could, they knelt down and took huge gulps. Quickly, they spit it out. The water was bitter and tasted awful! God knew they were thirsty. All He wanted was for them to pray to Him. Instead, they became afraid and cried to Moses, their leader. Moses knew what God wanted, so he began to talk to God. Beside the bitter water was a tree, and God told Moses to throw it in the water. When he obeyed, the water became sweet, and the people were able to drink. God had given them water for life. It was free, and all they had to do was come and drink. There were other times God's people needed water, but always there was enough, for God took care of them in everything.

There was a time when Jesus was tired and thirsty from walking. He sat down by a well and asked a woman who had come to draw water for a drink. He told her He could give her living water with which she would never be thirsty again. She thought He meant water to drink, but He was talking about the gift of eternal life. This gift comes from believing and trusting in Jesus.

Remember the tree Moses threw into the bitter water to make it sweet? There was another tree, a tree that was made into a cross. Jesus was hung on that tree and died for us. By dying for us, He gave us life and made everything sweet. When we come and give our lives to Him, joy will bubble up inside us, just like a spring of living water.

Questions:
Were the people thirsty?
Who gave them water?
How can we get the living water?

Prayer: Dear Lord, we want your living water. Give us Your joy inside, like a fountain bubbling over. Amen.

The Water of Life
(ADULTS)

Scriptures: Exodus 15:22-27; Jeremiah 2:13; Matthew 5:6; John 4:5-15, 7:37, 38; Revelation 22:17

Devotion: Water is found in many places in the desert. However, much of it is undrinkable, and so were the bitter waters of Marah encountered by the Israelites on their wilderness journey. The maximum time the human body can go without water in the desert is three days, and in this desperate situation, God's people seemed destined to die. Yet, in what seems a hopeless situation, God always provides. Directing Moses to a tree, God told him to throw the wood into the water. By doing this, the water became sweet, and the people could drink.

Surely God knew about the water, but why would He lead them there to drink of such bitterness? It makes no sense unless it is part of a higher plan. God wanted to test their commitment to Him, and by obeying Him, God would heal them. The children of Israel, however, could not see that a few more steps of faith would lead them to a place called Elim where there were twelve fresh springs to drink from. Instead of praying, they grumbled and missed God's healing purpose for their lives.

We live in a world desperately thirsty for living water, and many are dying of thirst. Needing love and acceptance, we deeply long for something to satisfy our inner cravings. We busily dig wells to try to earn salvation and thirst after the surface waters of materialism, greed, and self-gratification. No matter how much God provides for us, we are never satisfied. We fail to see the spring of living water, God's grace, flowing freely for anyone who will come and drink.

How can we obtain this living water? We need to realize that our thirst is a reflection of our own spiritual dryness which can only be quenched by thirsting after righteousness. We must allow God to break our willful spirits, so that His Spirit may enter our lives. In the Garden of Gethsemane, Jesus confessed that He did not want to drink the bitter cup, yet He surrendered to God's will. Because of His sacrificial obedience on the cross, the living water is available to anyone who stoops to drink. We must trust God to decide the time, place, and manner of testing that is best for us. Finally, we must remember that for every Marah, there is an Elim just beyond. After the crucifixion came the glorious resurrection. From this assurance of eternal life, living water will flow.

Prayer: Water of Life, we have tried the wells of the world, without satisfaction. We know only You can quench our thirsty souls. We come to drink of Your free gift and ask You to create an ever-flowing spring within us, renewing us each day to seek Your will in our lives. Amen.

Bread of Life

Symbol: a jar of manna

Memory Verses: "I am the Bread of Life. He who comes to me will never go hungry." John 6:35 (NIV)

"Do not work for food that spoils, but for food that endures to eternal life, which the Son of Man will give you." John 6:27 (NIV)

Songs to Sing:
  "Grumblers"
  "Guide Me, O Thou Great Jehovah"
  "Seek Ye First the Kingdom of God"

Bread of Life
(CHILDREN)

Scriptures: Exodus 16:1-5, 13-16, 31-35; John 6: 48-51

Devotion: Have you ever smelled baked bread fresh from the oven? It fills up the kitchen with happy feelings, doesn't it? What about your favorite sandwich with that good bread wrapped around it? Eating it just seems to warm your tummy inside, making you feel good all over. But what would happen to that sandwich without the bread? It would fall apart, and most of it would get on your hands, or worse, on the floor. Neither you nor your mother would be very happy about that. You'd get all grumpy, and you'd still be hungry!

God had told the children of Israel to trust Him. But they had run out of food in the wilderness, and they were hungry! Everything was falling apart! No sooner did their stomachs grumble than their mouths began to grumble. They cried, "Lord, we're hungry! Give us something to eat, and we want it now!" He didn't like their grumbling, but God didn't want His children to be hungry. So the next morning, little flakes of white food rained down from heaven and covered the ground. The people asked, "What is it? Are we supposed to eat this?" It was the special bread that God had given them to eat, and each day, they were to trust Him to send more.

Jesus said He was the Bread of Life, and if anyone ate of that bread, they would live forever. I'm sure the people who heard Him must have thought, "What is this? Are we supposed to eat Jesus?" What do you think Jesus meant? Jesus didn't mean for us to take a chunk out of His arm and eat it. But He does want us to think about Him like we think about bread. God holds everything together. When something good happens, it is His love that wraps around us, filling us with joy inside. When we are sad, it is that same Love that helps us feel better. And just like the "what is it" bread, He is all we need.

Jesus taught His disciples to pray, "Give us this day our daily bread." Everyday, we are to come asking and trusting that He will give us "His" bread. The next time we complain that we are hungry, let us remember Jesus is the Bread of Life, and He will take care of us. And when we do eat that good sandwich, let us thank Him for giving not only the sandwich but also Himself, so that we will be full of His Love forever!

Questions:
   Who gives us our food?
   Instead of complaining, will you thank Him for every thing?
   Who is the Bread of Life?

Prayer: "Our Father who art in heaven ..."
   A Lenten Activity: Make homemade bread (see Appendix).

Bread of Life
(ADULTS)

Scriptures: Exodus 16; John 6:22-58; Psalm 4, 27:13; Philippians 4:4-13

Devotion: The children of Israel needed food, and so they were provided with the gift of manna, raining from heaven. To test their obedience, God told them to gather only enough for their daily needs. But the Israelites were not satisfied with receiving just what they needed. They wanted more. They were grumblers, a people of endless ungrateful complaining.

Are we not often like these pilgrims in the wilderness? When we encounter danger, inconvenience, or difficult circumstances, are we prone to complain bitterly? We know that God loves us. We know of His promises, but somehow we can't seem to focus on trusting Him. Instead, we bull-doze ourselves forward, paying no attention to what God is telling us to do. Yearning for immediate happiness, we complain about having to wait for God's purpose to be fulfilled. We settle into the world's view of delusion and skepticism, simply because it's easier to doubt and complain.

How can we break this habit of grumbling? How can we trust Him when we don't feel He is meeting what we need or want in our lives? We first must realize we cannot solve life's everyday problems by ourselves. We will be too over-whelmed, and bitterness will eat away at us. We must not yearn for experiences of the past, for they will rot like the manna if we rely on them instead of Christ. The answer is simply resting in Jesus, the Bread of Life. We must come to Christ daily for His grace, not trusting in yesterday's strength or in what remains over. Taking one step of faith at a time, we will find that He is all we need.

The Lord commanded the Israelites to keep a jar of manna as a reminder of how God had provided for them in their everyday needs. Once you are out of your wilderness, don't forget the goodness God showed you there and how He sustained you. Today, on your Lenten journey, stop and remember God's goodness to you. Give up complaining, and eat of the Bread. Hunger for Him. When you put Him first over all things, then you will know true contentment, no matter what the circumstance.

Prayer: Jesus, we hunger for You. Just as the disciples heard and began to eat the bread, may we take You, our Bread of Life, to meet all our needs. Forgive us when we grumble or have less than a grateful heart about where we are, and help us see Your abundance in our everyday moments. Supply us with Your grace. It will sustain us in everything. Amen.

The Bronze Snake on a Pole

Symbol: a bronze snake and pole

Memory Verse: "When I am lifted up [on the cross], I will draw everyone to me." John 12:32 (TLB)

Songs to Sing:
   "Lift High the Cross"
   "My Faith Looks Up to Thee"
   "Turn Your Eyes Upon Jesus"

The Bronze Snake on a Pole
(CHILDREN)

Scriptures: Numbers 21:4-9; John 3:14-17; Romans 6:23

Devotion: (Show symbol) When you see this snake, what does it make you think about? (Adam and Eve, scary, poisonous, etc.) Let me tell you a story from the Bible that had to do with a lot of bad snakes, and one very special good snake. The children of Israel were complaining about how they had to eat the same food every day and how they were a long way from their home. They began pouting and saying ugly things about Moses and God. There were some poisonous snakes in the desert, and the snakes began to bite them. Many of them got very sick and were dying.

The people went to Moses and told him they were sorry they had been bad. They asked him to pray to God to take away the bad snakes. Even though the people had been ugly to Moses, he forgave them and began to pray for them. God heard his prayers and told him to make a snake out of brass and to put it on a pole. Moses was to lift the pole with the snake high enough for everyone to see it.

God told Moses the only thing the people had to do was to keep their eyes on the bronze snake. If they looked at the bad snakes, they would die, but if they looked at the good snake, they would get well again.

Have you ever pouted about anything? Doing something wrong can make us feel very bad, can't it? It almost makes us feel sick inside. When we do wrong, what do we need to do? All we need to do is to tell God that we are very sorry and then look to Jesus to forgive us and take away that sick feeling. And you know what? He will! That's why Jesus died on the cross, so we could be well again. Let's thank Him for this great love!

Questions:
How were the people bad?
How were they punished?
What did Moses make?

What did the people have to do to be healed?

Prayer: Dear Jesus, we are sorry when we complain or pout about things we have to do. Please forgive us and help us to look to You to take away our bad feelings. Thank you for being willing to be put on a cross to die for us, so we could be well again. Amen.

A Lenten Activity: This would be a great time to talk with your children about any people they have hurt by complaining words or actions. Going to the person and asking for forgiveness can be a humbling but a very important growing experience. Who knows? Maybe some of us adults should do this activity too!

The Bronze Snake on a Pole
(ADULTS)

Scriptures: Numbers 21:4-9; John 3:14-17, 6:40, 12:32; Romans 6:23; II Kings 18:4; Psalm 121

Devotion: Life was not going as well as the children of Israel wanted it to. They were wandering around in the hot desert, eating the same food over and over again (even if it was food of the angels), and wanting quick fixes on everything. Discouragement arose, and complaints against Moses and God were heard throughout the camp. God chose to bring judgment upon His people by allowing fiery snakes to bite them, causing pain, thirst, fever, and ultimately—death. Realizing they could not save themselves, the Israelites asked Moses to intercede to God to remove the snakes.

Sometimes God does not take away problems in the way we want Him to, and in this event, He devised an unusual plan for salvation. By shaping a bronze snake on a pole and lifting it up, freedom from death would come. Healing came not from the sight of the serpent but from looking upward to it in faith.

The devil's bite is sin and the effect is death. So must the Son of Man be lifted up on the cross to heal us from the deadly and destructive nature of sin. Though he was of the flesh, He was without sin and therefore crushed the Serpent's head. Anyone who looks up and sees Him with eyes of faith will be drawn to Him and gain eternal healing.

Too often, like the children of Israel, we look to the event or miracle instead of to the Miracle Maker. It is interesting to note that the bronze serpent Moses had made remained with the children of Israel until the time of King Hezekiah. Seeing that the Israelites had been burning incense to the Nehushtan, or the bronze serpent, Hezekiah had it broken into pieces. Let us not look to manmade miracles or events but to Jesus Christ, our Redeemer, who gives us life.

Prayer: Dear God, our hearts are tormented by the sin in our lives, causing us much grief and pain. We want You to save us, but in our way, not Your way. Forgive us of this. The ransom has already been paid for our sins; we just have to believe in You. Help us to lean not unto our own understanding but to look to You with eyes of faith. Amen.

DAY TWELVE

The Veil

Symbol: A veil or curtain

Memory Verse: "We have confidence to enter the Most Holy Place by the blood of Jesus, by a new and living way opened for us through the curtain, that is, his body."
Hebrews 10:19-20 (NIV)

Songs to Sing:
  "'Tis Finished! The Messiah Dies"
  "Spirit of Faith Come Down"
  "Nothing Between"

The Veil
(CHILDREN)

Scriptures: Exodus 26:31-34; Matthew 27:50,51; Romans 8:38; Hebrews 10:19-20

Devotion: What if someone told you that God was in the next room, and you couldn't talk to Him? You had to tell your minister or your parents what you wanted to say, and they would go through the door and talk to God for you. You couldn't hear God, see God, or know if He really understood you. That would be terrible, wouldn't it?

A long time ago, God told the children of Israel to build a special place for Him. This special place was called a tabernacle. It looked like a great big tent, and they carried it with them wherever they went. There was a special room inside the tabernacle where God would come to visit. But a great curtain was hung in front of the room, so no one could see inside. Only a special priest called the High Priest could enter the room through the curtain, and he could only go in one time a year. The people had to give their offerings and prayers to the priest, and then the priest would take them into the room to God. This happened for many years.

When Jesus lived on earth, the children of Israel had replaced the tabernacle with a beautiful temple to worship in. There was still the special room with the curtain hanging in front to keep out all the people. The people were still separated from God. But something happened on the day Jesus died. Let's read about it. (Matthew 27:50-51). The curtain was torn apart from top to bottom! Now, anyone who wanted to come and talk with God could walk right through the curtain.

Today, we go to our church building with our family and friends to worship. We listen to the minister or hear someone pray. The best thing is that we can pray, too. When we want to say something to God, we can stop wherever we are and talk to Him. It can be in our bed, in a car, on the beach, or even in a tree! If we are sad because someone has done something wrong to us or we have done something wrong, we can go right to God and tell Him how sorry we are. If we want to thank Him for a special blessing, we can praise Him right then. There is no curtain that stops us from being with God.

Questions:
> Who was in the special room of the tabernacle?
> What was hanging in front of the room?
> Who could go into the room?
> Why can we talk to God now?
> We can talk to God anytime because He loves to listen to our prayers. Would you like to talk to him right now?

Prayer: (This is a special time for your children to share with God any praises, hurts, or dreams. Let them think of things to say.) Thank You that we can come to You. In Jesus name we pray. Amen.

A Lenten Activity: Read "Behold the Savior of Mankind" written by Samuel Wesley. This may be found in *The United Methodist Hymnal.*

The Veil
(ADULTS)

Scriptures: Exodus 26:31-34, 40:3; Matthew 27:50-51; II Corinthians 3:7-18; Romans 8:22-38; Ephesians 2:13-18; Hebrews 4:16, 9:8-10, 10:19-20

Devotion: "If I had only known" is a phrase said by most of us at some point in our lives. We wish we would have had a crystal ball in choosing that perfect mate or career or in making those big decisions that proved to be disasters. Seeing into the future, however, means gaining insight into everything—all our joys and heartaches, all our accomplishments and failures. Realizing we can barely cope with the present trials, our "I wish I knew" quickly turns to "So glad I didn't know."

In Exodus 40:3, Moses is told to shield the Ark of the Covenant from the people with a veil, or curtain. God was not only protecting the Ark but His people as well, for He knew it would be impossible for them to fully understand and appreciate what was to come—the glory of the New Covenant. The people only saw the temporary sacrifices, imposed on them by the sacrificial system. They could not see the eternal future, which would be offered when God would send His only Son as the Final, Perfect Sacrifice.

Times of discipline and experiences in the wilderness prepared the Israelites to realize that any daily sacrifices brought to the temple and gifts offered were only temporary ways to gain forgiveness. However, as long as the old tabernacle stood with the veil in place, the ceremonial laws and the Old Covenant remained.

In Matthew, we read that the veil in the temple was torn in two from top to bottom as Christ's body hung on the cross. Christ, the Author and Finisher of our faith, ended the Old Covenant and established the New Covenant forever. Eternal life and freedom from sin lay concealed until the veil of Christ's body was torn and broken for us. Christ's death unveiled the mysteries of the Old Testament and revealed a new and living way to God, a way entered only by His blood. He died to bring us to God, and now, through Him, we may boldly and confidently approach the throne of grace.

Prayer: God, we come boldly before You, acknowledging that You are All Knowing and All Powerful. We are so glad we are on this side of the cross where Your plan has been revealed and completed before us. Help us to trust in You with all our hearts and to lean not unto our own understandings. Remove any veils that separate us from Your Love and from loving others. We pray this through the blood of Your Son, Jesus Christ. Amen.

The Tabernacle

Symbol: a tabernacle

Memory Verse: "Here I am! I stand at the door, and knock. If anyone hears my voice and opens the door, I will come in and eat with him, and he with me." Revelation 3:20 (NIV)

Songs to Sing:
   "I Am the Church"
   "Surely the Presence of the Lord Is in This Place"
   "Lord Prepare Me to Be a Sanctuary"
   "Behold, Behold, I Stand at the Door and Knock"

The Tabernacle
(CHILDREN)

Scriptures: Exodus 25:1, 8-9; Revelation 3:3

Devotion: Do you remember the tabernacle we talked about last time? God wanted Moses to build this tabernacle. It would be a place where God could come and visit His people. God wanted this to be a very special place, so He gave them special orders on how to build it. The furniture was placed in a certain way, and only a special person called the high priest was allowed to go into certain areas. God told His people to bring things from their homes that were valuable to help build the tabernacle. The people brought money, clothing material, perfumes, and even their jewelry to be used. They gave these things to God, and then they helped Moses build the beautiful tabernacle. After it was built, God came and visited the people in a cloud by day and a cloud of fire by night. The tabernacle was placed in the very center of Israel's camp, and the people lived around it. Every day, they would bring sacrifices and gifts to be offered to Him.

God had the tabernacle built in a certain way to show how Christ would work in our lives one day. Now, you are the place where God lives. Your prayers and praises are the daily gifts you can give to Him. Your body is the tabernacle, and He wants you to take good care of it. Jesus also wants to live in your tabernacle, but He is a gentleman. He will not come in unless you ask Him to. When you open the door of your life to Him, He will come in and never leave you.

Questions:
   What did the people bring?
   Why did they bring these things?
   Who is the church?
   Who wants to come in and live forever?

Prayer: (For the nonbeliever) Jesus, I need You in my life. Forgive me for my sins and come into my heart. You are the only way I can be happy with God. I open the door to You. Thank You for coming in. Amen.

(For the believer) Jesus, thank You for being in my life. I know that I am Your church and You live in me. Help me each day to clean my life from any ugly thought that might come in. I bring You my love and praise You for loving me. Amen.

A Lenten Activity: Show the painting of Jesus knocking at the door. Have your children pay close attention to the door. The door has no doorknob and can only be opened from the inside.

Make a tabernacle jar. Have your children give up something each day during Lent and put the money they have saved in the jar. Just as the children of Israel did, they can bring their gift to the church and present it to the Lord on Easter Day.

The Tabernacle
(ADULTS)

Scriptures: Exodus 25:1-40; John 1:14, 2:19-22; Ephesians 2:19-22; Hebrews 8–9; Revelation 3:20, 11:19, 21:3

Devotion: In reading the scriptures about the holy tabernacle and the specific furniture to be placed in it, we see a detailed picture of the Redeemer to come (Hebrews 8:5). There was only one tabernacle, and it was the means of uniting the Israelites in their worship to the true and living God. Christ is the only way to God. The Outer Court held the bronze altar where burnt offerings were sacrificed. Christ is our sin offering. The priests cleansed themselves at the laver before entering the holy place to render their daily services.

We are washed clean by Christ's blood to live for Him and others. In the Holy Place was the golden lampstand, typifying Christ as the Light of the World. The table of sacred bread represents Christ as the Bread of Life, and the golden altar of incense signifies Christ interceding for us constantly before God. Behind the veil, which represents the body of Christ, is the Holy of Holies where the Ark of the Covenant is placed, and only the High Priest could enter. Christ, our High Priest, has entered the heavenly tabernacle, heaven, with the final atonement, the shedding of His blood on the cross. Because of this great and final sacrifice, believers may enter boldly and confidently into the presence of God.

The tabernacle was the place where God dwelt among His people. In John 1:14 we read, "the Word (Jesus) became flesh and dwelt among us—full of grace and truth." In A.D. 70, the tabernacle was destroyed. No longer were the items in the temple needed because Christ's death ended the sacrificial system for which they were created. The true Light had come into the world. As Christ came to draw us into fellowship with God, our bodies have now become the tabernacle in which the Holy Spirit dwells. God has provided the atonement by which our lives can be cleansed. The altar and table of sacred bread is now free to us because we are priests to Him serving Him daily. Leaving the world behind, let us enter into fellowship with our Father, offering our prayers, our lives, and our love to the Perfect Builder of our faith.

Prayer: I offer my life as a living sacrifice to You. May I no longer be conformed to the pattern of the world but be molded into a tabernacle holy and pleasing to You. Renew my mind daily so that I may know Your perfect will and may serve you in a way that is pleasing to You. May your presence shine through the windows of my life so that others will be drawn to you. Amen.

Christ, the Rock

Symbol: a rock

Memory Verse: "The LORD is my rock and my fortress."
Psalm 18:2 (KJV)

Songs to Sing:
  "The Wise Man and the Foolish Man"
  "My Hope Is Built"
  "His Name Is Wonderful"

Christ, the Rock
(CHILDREN)

Scriptures: Exodus 17:1-6; Psalm 18:2; Matthew 7:24-27; I Corinthians 10:4

Devotion: God had taken care of the children of Israel. No longer slaves in Egypt, the children were being led to a beautiful place where they could live happily with their families. God had provided water, manna, and even a cloud of fire to lead them during the journey. But the children still grumbled when they came to another place without water. Once more Moses cried to the Lord. The Lord told him to hit a rock with his staff, and when Moses obeyed, water gushed out of it for the people to drink. Let's read who this Rock is (I Corinthians). It is Jesus! From Him the Living Water flows and all people who drink are saved.

Jesus wants us to depend on Him to be strong, just like a rock. He liked to tell stories and one day, He told a story about two men who built some houses. A foolish man built his house on some sand while the other man, a very wise man, dug down very deep and built his house on a strong rock. One day, it rained very hard, and all the sand was washed away. The foolish man's house fell down, but the house on the rock was safe. The rock would not wash away because it was strong and would last forever! The wise man knew he was safe!

Jesus is the Rock we should build our lives on. He also wants to be the Rock that our home and church are built on. When we trust in Christ, we are being very smart! Our Rock not only protects and takes care of us but also provides everything we need.

Questions:
Who is the Rock?
What happened to the house on the sand?
What happened to the house on the rock?

Prayer: Jesus thank You for being the Rock. We know we

can run to You and You will protect us. You are strong and will always be there for us. Help us to build our lives and our church on You, the Solid Rock. Amen.

A Lenten Activity: If possible, experiment with God's wonders and play in the sand today. Build some sandcastles and act out the story of the Wise and Foolish Man. Make a sand-painting with the words "Jesus is the Rock" on it.

Christ, the Rock
(ADULTS)

Scriptures: Exodus 17:1-6; Psalm 18:2; Matthew 7:24-27, 16:13-18; I Corinthians 3:10-18, 10:4; I Peter 1:4-8

Devotion: Christ asks His disciples, "Who do you think I am?" Like Peter, we reply, "You are the Christ, the son of the living God." It is this profession of faith by which we begin to build our lives on. Christ, the sure foundation, sustains and holds us up, as a house upon a rock. Christ, seen as our Rock, is firm, solid, and immovable. He will not fail us nor deceive us, and the one who trusts in Him will never be foolish. We cling to The Rock—

To go up. Looking to the higher Rock, we climb to be enthroned in God's presence and to share in His glory forever. We rejoice that we have a stronghold, His Spirit, working in us to sanctify our natures unto Him.

To find sustenance. The rock in the wilderness gave spiritual water for the Israelites' salvation. So Christ is the Rock from which we are spiritually refreshed.

To find refuge. He is our safe and secure place of retreat from the world. When there is loneliness, disappointment, or weariness, we go the Rock, and He will shield us.

To stay secure. Drenched by the rains of life's trials, we cling to the promise of Romans 8:28 that "that all things work together for good to them that love God." Numbers 24:21 also promises that our dwelling place is secure if our nest is set in the Rock.

To go down into the world. Since we have heard the Word, we now respond to the Word. Holding on to the Rock, we reach out to show others how to build their lives on the foundation of Jesus Christ. Part of our responsibility as Christians is to help others stop and think about where their lives are headed and to point out the consequences of ignoring the Rock, as the foolish man did.

What's important in your life? Who or what are you building on for security and happiness? Is it religion, wealth, relationships, or Christ? One day, the quality of each man's work will be revealed. Let us cling to the hope of Christ, the Sure Foundation, so that when our work is shown for what it is, we will be called wise men.

Prayer: Christ, my Rock, I trust You to lift my spirits upward to You. I trust You to be my Companion. I trust You to keep me from sin. I trust You to help me rest in You. I trust You to give me a sense of purpose for others. When all earthly things have passed away, I trust Your foundation will remain standing. Amen.

Jesus, Our High Priest

Symbol: a priest

Memory Verse: "Let us therefore come boldly unto the throne of grace, that we may obtain mercy, and find grace to help in time of need." Hebrews 4:16 (KJV)

Songs to Sing:
   "Love Divine, All Loves Excelling"
   "Sweet Hour of Prayer"
   "Blessed Assurance"
   "Jesus Loves the Little Children"

Jesus, Our High Priest
(CHILDREN)

Scriptures: Exodus 28:41-42, 30:10; Hebrews 8:11, 9:6-7, 11-15, 24-28

Devotion: Isn't it great that we can talk to God about everything? When something good happens, we can thank Him for His blessings, or when we are hurting because someone has been unkind to us, we can go straight to Him and talk to Him about it. Did you know we would not be able to do that if Jesus had not come to earth to die for us? Someone else would have to talk to Him for us. That's what the children of Israel had to do.

(Show the symbol) God was teaching His people how to worship Him. He needed priests to take care of the tabernacle and to give gifts to God. These priests had to be members of a special family, the Levites, and Aaron would be the high priest, the one in charge of all the other priests. The priests would represent the people before God and were commanded to live holy lives.

Do you remember the Ark of the Covenant? This was the chest where God would come to visit. It had been placed in a very special room of the church, but only one person was allowed in the room. Aaron, the high priest, could come in and offer the sacrifice to God. Once each year, Aaron would put on special clean clothes and enter this holy room. He would sprinkle the blood of an animal on the mercy seat and pray to God for the people. On Aaron's clothes were special stones with the names of the families of Israel engraved on them. Even though the people could not go in, their names were shown before God as the priest prayed their prayers for them. The priest stood between God and the people.

Christ came to the earth and died for us. But do you know where He is now? He rose from the grave, went to heaven, and is sitting beside God right now talking to Him about us. He is now our High Priest. Let's read about this in the Bible (Hebrews 9:11-15). This means that when Christ entered the Most Holy Place in heaven to be with God, He brought the last sacrifice ever. He brought His blood shed on the cross. Now, we can talk to God through Christ, and we don't need anyone else to do it for us. We can pray and praise Him anytime.

Questions:
Who was the only one who could come to God for the people?
Who is our High Priest?
What was His sacrifice?

Prayer: Lord, enter my heart and hear my prayer. (Pray for personal needs and thanksgivings.)
Thank You that we can come and talk to You anytime we want. Thank You for letting us know You. Amen.

Jesus, Our High Priest
(ADULTS)

Scriptures: Exodus 28–29, 30:6-10; Hebrews 4:14-16, 7:22-28, 8-10:18; John 17

Devotion: The sacrificial system was provided as a way for the people of Israel to obtain God's forgiveness. Because of their sin, the Israelites could not approach God. Their only access to Him was through a mediator, the high priest, who would offer a sacrifice and use the animal's blood to atone first for his own sins and then for the sins of the people. Precious stones, sewn on the priestly garment, were engraved with the names of the twelve tribes of Israel. The priest would enter the Holy of Holies, symbolically carrying the burden of all His people on his shoulders as he represented the nation before God.

Today, neither mediating priests nor the sacrificing of animals is required because our High Priest, Jesus Christ, has come. We can now go directly to God through Christ. He is our access to God because He has been on both sides. As a human representative who understands all our weaknesses, He intercedes for us before God. As God's representative, pure and without sin, He assures us of God's forgiveness. Christ has gone before us. He has entered the heavenly kingdom on our behalf, and because His sacrifice is finished, He is seated beside God. He is not only at God's side, however, but is on our side as well. Christ is in God's presence at all times, constantly pleading for mercy and grace in our times of need. In return, God is personally available to all who offer their love and faith to Him. Relationship has been restored, and we now have unlimited access to God. We may approach the throne of grace, confident of our special union with God through Christ.

The High Priestly Prayer of Christ, found in John 17, is a prayer for unity. First, Christ prays for Himself. With no need of cleansing and His work completed, Christ asks to be unified and restored to His heavenly position with God. He then prays for the protection of His disciples and for their joy, which only comes from living in a close union with Christ. Finally, He prays for all present and future believers. Christ knows every believer and intercedes for each as a precious child of God. He is constantly praying for all believers to become as one, so His perfect love may be seen by all. May we strive to follow this High Priest's example of holy living, unified by His Love.

Prayer: God, we are so glad we can come to You with all our thoughts, fears, failures, and desires. Help us to see where we may cause disunity with others, and give us the wisdom to find avenues for unity with those who disagree with us. Help others to see Your love within our lives. We come to You through Jesus Christ, our Lord. Amen.

Jonah and the Fish

Symbol: a big fish

Memory Verse: "In my distress I called to the LORD, and he answered me." Jonah 2:2 (NIV)

Songs to Sing:
   "I Wonder How It Felt"
   "Christ Arose"
   "He Lifted Me"

Jonah and the Fish
(CHILDREN)

Scriptures: Jonah 1-2; Matthew 12:40

Devotion: (Show symbol) Do you remember a story about a man and a big fish like this in the Bible? There once was a man named Jonah who had said "No!" to something God wanted him to do. He got into a big boat and tried to get as far away from God as he could. But a big storm came upon the waters, and Jonah was thrown into the sea.

It looked like Jonah was going to die, but God had a different plan. He sent a huge fish to swallow Jonah without hurting him, and Jonah stayed inside the fish for three days and nights! I bet it was dark and scary inside that fish, but do you know what Jonah did? He prayed to the Lord, and at the Lord's command, the fish spit Jonah onto dry land. Jonah was alive, and after that day, he told many people about what had happened to him. Because Jonah was willing to share his story, many people turned to the Lord.

Every time we look at this fish, let's remember that although it looked like Jonah was dead, he really wasn't. We can also remember when Jesus was put in the tomb, it looked like Jesus was dead, but He was really alive. On the third day, He arose from His grave and because of that miracle, we too can come to know and to love Him!

Questions:
    What did the fish do?
    How long was Jonah inside the fish?
    How long was Jesus inside the earth before he arose?

Prayer: Dear Lord, whenever I am scared, help me to remember the story of Jonah. Thank you for saving him, and saving me, so that I can tell others about how much You love us. Amen.

Jonah and the Fish
(ADULTS)

Scriptures: Psalm 40:2; Jonah 1:17–2:10; Matthew 12:38-41, 16:4; Luke 11:29-32

Devotion: Just like the people of Jesus' time, we demand that Christ show us great miracles. We want to see instant healings, mountains moved, and amazing phenomenons proving He is truly the resurrected Son of God. Jesus simply reminds us of the evidence God has already given, a symbol of what was to happen in His death and resurrection. The sign was Jonah in the belly of the fish.

In Jonah 1:17, we see the Lord provided a fish to swallow Jonah. From the beginning of time, God has planned every event to prepare us to understand the miracle of the Resurrection. It is not mere coincidence that just as Jonah was in the belly for three days, so was Christ in the heart of the earth. God is in control of everything.

As God saved Jonah from the depths of death to bring redemption, Christ was lifted up to bring about the repentance of many. The people of Nineveh repented at the sign of Jonah. May we turn from our own wills and trust in the Resurrection, the breaking of sin's power over us.

"O Love that wilt not let me go,
I rest my weary soul in thee;
I give thee back the life I owe,
That in thine ocean depths its flow may richer, fuller be."

Prayer from Jonah 2:2-9 (NIV): "In my distress I called to the LORD, and he answered me. From the depths of the grave I called for help, and you listened to my cry. You hurled me into the deep, into the very heart of the seas, and the currents swirled about me; all your waves and breakers swept over me. I said, 'I have been banished from your sight; yet I will look again toward your holy temple.' The engulfing waters threatened me, the deep surrounded me; seaweed was wrapped around my head. To the roots of the mountains I sank down; the earth beneath barred me in forever.

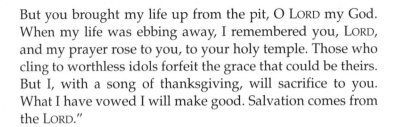

But you brought my life up from the pit, O LORD my God. When my life was ebbing away, I remembered you, LORD, and my prayer rose to you, to your holy temple. Those who cling to worthless idols forfeit the grace that could be theirs. But I, with a song of thanksgiving, will sacrifice to you. What I have vowed I will make good. Salvation comes from the LORD."

The Scapegoat

Symbol: a goat

Memory Verses: "As far as the east is from the west, so far has he removed our transgressions from us." Psalm 103:12 (NIV)

"He himself bore our sin, so that we might die to sin and live for righteousness." I Peter 2:24 (NIV)

Songs to Sing:
  "For God So Loved the World"
  "Jesus Walked This Lonesome Valley"
  "I Must Tell Jesus"

The Scapegoat
(CHILDREN)

Scriptures: Leviticus 16:5-10, 20-22; Psalm 103:12; John 1:29; Hebrews 8:12

Devotion: We have read how on the Day of Atonement, an animal was killed and its blood was sprinkled on the Ark of the Covenant. Do you remember why the Priest did this? The blood covered the sins of the people, and God could forgive them. But even though God had forgiven their sins, He knew the people would feel guilty for what they had done. When you do something wrong, have you ever felt like that? You have a hurt inside that just doesn't seem to go away. So, God thought of a way to not only forgive us, but to "forget" the bad things we do, so we won't be sad anymore.

On that same Day of Atonement, there also was another animal that was to be brought to the altar of the church. This animal was a young goat, but this goat would not be killed like the other one. Instead, the Priest would lay his two hands on the head of the goat and would tell all the bad things the people of Israel had done and how sorry they were. By doing this, he was putting all the sins of the people on the goat's head. After that, the goat was taken outside the camp and left alone in the wilderness, a dangerous place where no one went. Because the goat was never seen again, it was just like God had "forgotten" the people had ever done wrong. He not only forgave but He removed their sins forever from His eyes.

That's the way it is with us. When we are truly sorry and tell God about what we have done wrong, God forgives us. And then He chooses to forget about it! It's a great feeling knowing our sins have been taken away, and He doesn't even remember we did them.

Let's go back to the goat in the wilderness. The goat was lonely because he was in a place where no one was and no one loved him. But he was willing to take the sins away.

When Jesus was on the cross, many people hated Him. But He was willing to put all our sins on Him, so we could be happy again. God loves us very much!

Questions:
  What did the people send out into the wilderness?
  Was the goat lonely?
  Does it make Jesus lonely and sad when you don't love Him?

Prayer: Dear Lord, thank You that You are willing to forgive us every day and choose to forget all the bad things we do. We are so happy You do this for us. Help us to live the same way by forgiving and forgetting when others do us wrong. Amen.

The Scapegoat
(ADULTS)

Scriptures: Leviticus 16:5-10, 20-22, 28; Isaiah 53:5-7; Romans 6; I Peter 2:21-25; Hebrews 8:12

Devotion: The deed is done. All the adultery, cheating, lying, and hate have been transferred from sinners to this Scapegoat. Many He has loved have abandoned Him and left Him to die. A cry rises forth, "My God, my God, why hast Thou forsaken me?" The Scapegoat realizes that His own Father has turned away. He feels utterly alone and deserted, crushed beneath the sins of the whole world.

How can we ever repay Him for what He has done? This gift of grace is something we are unworthy to receive. What can we do or say to take away our guilt for piercing Him with our insults and pride? Even though God has forgiven us, we can't forgive ourselves. What do we do?

His eyes, filled with tears of blood and loneliness, look

down to us from the cross with the answer. He requires nothing, for you are valuable in just who you are. He could not bear the thought of you having to face the penalty of death alone, and so this Scapegoat became our "escape" as He paid a price, the price of Himself. All He asks is that you bring your sin, lay it upon Him, and receive the free gift of atonement. He has taken away your sins to remember them no more.

This mercy is difficult to comprehend, but it is no reason to take back the burden of our sin and to wander aimlessly in a wilderness of frustration and hurt. Acceptance of God's gift is the only way to rid us of the loneliness and pain that comes from being away from God.

In the first chapter of Leviticus, God requires every man to bring an offering unto the Lord. We must personally bring our all to Him. All our evil desires and love of sin must be placed upon Him. In so doing, we will no longer be slaves to sin and guilt but servants to Christ. There will still be wildernesses to travel but no more loneliness. We are now bound to One Who loves us.

Prayer: Our Lord, You bore the punishment we deserved. You became sin. Help us to receive this gift. We cannot bear separation from You, and so we confess our sins, laying all our pride and selfishness upon You. We know that You are faithful and just to forgive us and to remember them no more. Our bondage to sin has been crucified, so that we may live for righteousness. Accompany us through the perilous journeys of whatever wilderness awaits us. Guide us by Your Holy Spirit.

Our Comforter

Symbol: a dove

Memory Verses: "He shall give you another Comforter, that he may abide with you for ever." John 14:16 (KJV)

"I will put my spirit within you." Ezekiel 36:27 (KJV)

Songs to Sing:
"Spirit Song"
"Blessed Quietness"
"Spirit of the Living God"
"Sweet, Sweet Spirit"

Our Comforter
(CHILDREN)

Scripture: Luke 3:21-22; John 14:16-17, 25-27; Romans 8:16

Devotion: There is only one true God, and yet, there are three Persons of God. The Bible tells us that there is God the Father, God the Son, and God the Holy Ghost or Spirit. God the Father is the Person who created us and who lives in heaven. God the Son is the Person who came to earth as a baby and died on the cross for us. On Easter, He arose and now He sits beside God in heaven. God the Holy Spirit is the one who lives today in our hearts if we believe in Jesus. God the Holy Spirit is the one who brings us peace and works with power in us to live good lives.

There was a special day when God showed Himself as the three Persons. It was the day when Jesus was baptized. Jesus and His cousin John went down into the Jordan River together. There John baptized Jesus with water. All of a sudden, the heavens opened up, and something that looked like a dove came down and rested on Jesus. Do you know who the dove was? He was God the Holy Spirit in the form of a dove. Jesus was showing us how we can become new people with the peace and power of the Holy Spirit to do God's will. At the very same time, a voice was heard from heaven that said, "You are my Son, whom I love; with you I am well pleased." It was the voice of God, the Father! He was telling Jesus and the world that He was very proud of His Son and that He loved Him very much. So you see, all three Persons were there: the Father, the Son, and the Holy Spirit.

For the next three years, Jesus did amazing things. By the Spirit, He healed people and forgave their sins. He baptized with the Holy Spirit and raised people from the dead. He died, but rose again, and went to be with His Father in heaven. Yet, He did not leave His disciples alone. He told them that God would send a Comforter to give them peace, just like God had sent Him the Holy Spirit as a dove. Jesus promises us this same Comforter, the Holy Spirit.

When you believe in Jesus, you become a new person. You become a child of God the Father. Your sins are forgiven because God the Son died for you. God the Holy Spirit comes and lives inside you to make you pure and holy. All three Persons work together, giving you a new heart that loves God and wants to do His will.

Questions:
Who is God the Son?
What did God the Father do when Jesus was baptized?
What did God the Holy Spirit do when Jesus was baptized?

Prayer: God, we thank You for the sign of the dove that makes us know you loved Jesus, Your Son. We know You are pleased with us also when we give our hearts to Jesus. May Your Spirit lead us just as He led Jesus. Amen.

Our Comforter
(ADULTS)

Scriptures: Psalm 51:10; Zephaniah 3:17; Luke 3:21-22; John 14:16-27, 15:26-27, 16:5-15; Romans 8:16; Philippians 4:7-13

Devotion: Psychologists say an overwhelming majority of core wounds patients seek healing for stem from some type of dysfunctional relationship within their home during childhood. Emotional abuse may have come from an overbearing or unforgiving father, a criticizing and unloving mother, or an absent parent. Whatever the reason, the emotional scars are perpetuated throughout the generations resulting in insecurity, self-doubt, loneliness, and shame. In contrast, those from loving homes recall how a comforting pat on the back or a cheering voice from the stands gave them the power to run faster, play better, or study harder.

Growing older, they excelled in life far beyond their own limitations, simply because they had heard the powerful words, "I love you and I am proud of you."

Christ came and was baptized out of obedience to His Father. In this act, God's voice was heard blessing His Son with His love for Him. Christ was assured of this love by the form of a dove descending upon Him, and from this peace of knowing His Father was well pleased came forth power: power to heal, teach, and forgive.

Jesus promised this same power to His disciples in a Counselor who would help them with their fears. This Comforter would never desert them and would give them a peace that the world cannot understand. Unlike worldly peace, which is usually defined as the absence of conflict, Christ promised a peace during conflict.

We cannot call the past back to do anything about it, but it is possible to become new people and to change from anything that was or has been before. Behind this newness of life must lie our acceptance of God's blessing, His forgiveness, and His ability to put His Spirit within us. We then are assured that we need never fear any circumstance that comes into our lives. This is why Christ came, bled, and died for us. If there had been no one else on this earth, God's plan would have been the same. We alone are worth saving. We alone are worth loving.

Is there someone in your life who needs a blessing today? One kind pat on the back or word of encouragement can "pass His peace" to a lonely child, a frustrated student, or an unhappy co-worker. Yield to the Comforter and power to bless will come.

Prayer: Holy Comforter, fill us with your peace and assurance that the Father is pleased with us. Counselor, teach us of Him and empower us to do His Will. Spirit of Truth, reveal today people who are in pain and need a blessing. Help us to "pass His peace." Amen.

Fishers of Men

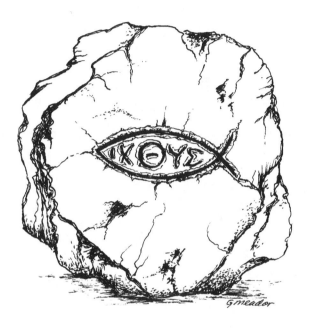

Symbol: a fish

Memory Verses: "Don't be afraid; from now on you will catch men." Luke 5:10 (NIV)

"Love the LORD your God . . . and serve him." Deuteronomy 11:13 (NIV)

Songs to Sing:
   "Fishers of Men"
   "Rise Up, O Men of God"
   "O Jesus, I Have Promised"

Fishers of Men
(CHILDREN)

Scriptures: Luke 5:1-11

Devotion: Do you know what this sign means? It is the sign of a Christian. The early Christians used this sign when they met each other. Today, people use this sign on their cars or in their businesses to tell others they belong to Christ. The sign of the fish is used everywhere simply because of some words Jesus said in the Bible. One day, Jesus was on the shore of the Sea of Galilee. There was a crowd of people following Him wanting to hear Him. Jesus saw some fishermen named Peter and Andrew beside their boat. He asked if they would take him out into the water. They did, and all the people could see and hear Jesus. Then He told Peter to go further out into the water to catch some fish. Peter was very tired because they had been working hard all night and had not caught anything! But he did what Jesus told him to do, and when they pulled their nets up from the water, there were so many fish, they couldn't count them! Their nets began to break, so they yelled to James and John, their friends in another boat, to help them. The boats became so full of fish they began to sink!

Peter fell on his knees in amazement at this miracle! He told Jesus to get away from him because he was a sinner and Jesus was too good to be around him. But Jesus kindly looked upon him and said, "Don't be afraid; from now on you will go fishing for men." Fishermen were hard workers and had to always be prepared to catch fish. Even when no fish were caught, they had to be patient because their family and friends needed fish to eat. Peter also knew being a fisher of men would not be easy, but he saw that Jesus believed in him. And so, he left his boat, along with Andrew, John, and James, and began to follow Him. He became one of the greatest fishers of men ever known!

Jesus wants all of us to be fishers of men. There are many people who have troubles and need to know God's love. It's up to us to throw our nets out to all the people we know and try to bring them to God. There are many ways to show we are Christians. We can use the symbol of the fish just like the first Christians did. We can go to church to praise God. We can talk to others and let others see by our actions how much Jesus means to us. If we obey and follow Him, we will truly be fishers of men.

Questions:
   What was Peter?
   What did he become when he followed Jesus?
   Will you follow Jesus?

Prayer: Jesus, I want to follow you like Peter did. Help me to be a fisher of men and to tell others about You in everything I do. Amen.

Fishers of Men
(ADULTS)

Scriptures: Luke 5:1-11; Acts 2:14–4:13

Devotions: A woman brings a chicken casserole to a new couple in town. Extending tired arms, young teenagers dangle puppets for a backyard Bible club. A successful businessman spends his free time driving a van for the elderly. A principal sends cheerful notes of encouragement to not only his staff but his students as well. A young girl, washing dishes in a soup kitchen one day, is seen another day scrubbing floors in an underprivileged school. An industrious worker gives his only means of livelihood, a boat, so that the word of God may be heard. All these people have something in common. They are fishers of men.

In selecting His disciples, Jesus saw Simon as a perfect candidate to catch men. Simon was willing to turn the only thing he had, his business, into a channel of service for Christ. With impossibility seeming evident, Simon obeyed Christ, steering his boat further into the water and leaving the rest to God. In so doing, he recognized his own sinfulness and that Christ alone provided the miracles. In humility and self-denial, Simon forsook all and began a new journey with Christ. In the book of Acts, we see the result of this changed man, Peter. Peter exclaims, "Silver and gold I do not have, but what I have I give you." No longer did he have a boat to be used, but he now used the confidence given by the Holy Spirit to speak up for Christ whenever he had the opportunity. Although he was an unschooled, ordinary fisherman, the people were amazed at what Jesus was doing through him.

Today, let's consider how we feel about this journey of fishing for men. We may not want to go. We may not want to give up the things in our lives that hinder us from following Christ. We may feel, like Peter, we have made so many bad mistakes that God could never forgive us. And if He did, we may feel we have nothing to offer, being ordinary people with no special abilities or successes to be used by Him. We do not know what the journey will require. We may run risks of rejection and even persecution in trying to win others to Christ. We may labor long and catch nothing. But leaving our past behind, let us see how God can use the most ordinary for His kingdom. Peter learned a new way of life, and so will we. Peter made mistakes, and so will we. Peter denied, and so will we. Peter learned to boldly confess, and so will we.

Prayer: O God, we would join Simon in following You and answering Your call. Give us the patience and perseverance to continue letting down our nets, even if we do not see success. Help us to be willing to allow You to work in our lives to save. Send us on our way. Amen.

Celebrating a Blessing

Symbol: a jar of water

Memory Verse: "Do whatever he tells you." John 2:5 (NIV)

Songs to Sing:
  "'Tis So Sweet to Trust in Jesus"
  "Praise God from Whom All Blessings Flow"
  "Rejoice in the Lord Always"

Celebrating a Blessing
(CHILDREN)

Scripture: John 2:1-11; I Thessalonians 5:16-18

Devotion: Jesus and His disciples had been invited to a wedding at Cana in Galilee. Mary, His mother, had come also, and there was great excitement. The wedding celebration went on for several days, and everyone was happy. But toward the end, they didn't have anything left to drink. This would be very embarrassing for the family, so Mary turned to Jesus for help. She had watched Him grow up as a child into a kind, good man, and she knew He could take care of any problem. She turned to the servants and told them to do whatever He said. She knew that if they obeyed Jesus, something good would happen.

There were six huge jars standing near the door. They were always filled with water to wash and clean the feet of those who entered the home. But, there had been so many guests at the wedding that all of the jars were empty. Jesus told the servants to fill them with water. The servants did not understand how this could help, but they obeyed Jesus. They filled the jars to the very top. He then told them to take some to the man in charge of the party. Once again the servants obeyed, and to their amazement, the drink was better than anyone had tasted at the party. The bridegroom didn't know where it had come from. But the servants knew. A miracle had happened! Jesus showed He can do anything because He is God who came down to save us and give us many blessings. When we believe in Jesus and obey Him, miracles will happen in our lives. Isn't He wonderful?

Today, let's think of ways we can obey God and celebrate in His blessings. Oh, how sweet to trust in Jesus and to know that when He says something, we can believe it will be done!

Questions:
What did Mary tell the servants to do?
What did Jesus tell the servants to do?
Can Jesus bless us when we obey Him?

Prayer: Jesus, You have given us so many blessings. Help us obey You every day. When we do, we know we will be happy. Amen.

A Lenten Activity: Have a celebration today! God's love for us is revealed in many ways. Celebrate the outdoors by taking a walk and seeing His miracles, or have a special dinner and play games with your family. Whatever You do, let your joy be full with the abundant life of Christ!

Celebrating a Blessing
(ADULTS)

Scriptures: John 2:1-11; Philippians 4:4-7; I Thessalonians 5:16-18

Devotion: There are times in life when it seems we have run out of "wine." An overwhelming problem or unexpected event brings emptiness within, like a hollow vessel. With no strength or energy to cope, we yearn for the sweetness of life. How can these times of discouragement result in the wine of celebration? From our emptiness, how can we be filled with the true joy and blessing from God? The miracle at Cana reveals the steps of how faith and obedience to Christ can bring celebration!

First, we must be honest with ourselves and trust God with those hurtful, agonizing parts of life. Hearing there was no wine left, Mary's immediate response was to turn to Christ. She cast her cares upon the Son, knowing He cared. Next, we are to obey. Without questioning, the servants simply followed the words of Christ. There will be times we will not understand the workings of God. But when we obey, genuine joy is produced. Without obedience, joy is hollow and artificial. When we bring to Him all of ourselves: our work, our knowledge, our relationships, and the events of our daily lives, He transforms us. We are changed into a sweet wine, perfected in His Love, and it is then that we begin to understand His purpose for our lives.

There is one more step to follow for celebration to occur. The servants at Cana were to draw some wine from the jars and give to the host. The wine would have been of no value unless shared with the guests. Our joy is incomplete without our willingness to share and serve the Living Water. Celebration comes when we empty ourselves, are filled with love and compassion, and take on a spirit of service for one another. If we submit to His will, we will taste the blessing that comes from following Christ.

Lent is a time for giving up and taking on. As Christians, we are to be anxious for nothing and cast all our cares upon Him. We will become joyful, that is, full of joy. And then, trusting in the miracle working power of Jesus, celebration will begin!

It is important to note that Christ's glorification was not to come in the providing of miracles, such as the changing of water into wine. The jars of water were used for ceremonial cleansings. Jesus' death would nullify the old methods of purification. The outpouring of his blood on the cross would offer a "new wine" to cleanse the believer forever. This would be His hour. This would be His glorification.

Prayer: God, our lives are like empty vessels without You. Fill us with the richness of Your Love. Let the substance of Your love in us flow out to bring strength and life to others. Amen.

Calming the Storm

Symbol: a boat

Memory Verse: "Whoever trusts in the LORD is kept safe." Proverbs 29:25 (NIV)

Songs to Sing:
   "Jesus Loves Me"
   "Through It All"
   "Jesus, Savior, Pilot Me"

Calming the Storm
(CHILDREN)

Scriptures: Proverbs 29:25; Matthew 8:23-27

Devotion: Are you afraid of anything? Who or where do you go so you can feel safe? You go to _____ because you know they love you, and they are going to take care of you. There was a time when the disciples were very afraid, and they forgot just how much Jesus loved them and how He had promised to take care of them.

One night, Jesus and His disciples got into a boat. Jesus was very tired, so He soon fell fast asleep. Suddenly, a great wind began to blow, and the little boat was caught up in a terrible storm! It was raining very hard, and the waves were rocking the boat back and forth. The disciples thought they were going to die! They remembered Jesus was asleep, so they ran and woke Him up. They were screaming because they were so scared. But Jesus was not afraid. He got up and shouted for the wind and the waves to stop. The wind died down to a gentle breeze, and the sea became very calm.

The disciples couldn't believe what they had seen. Here was a man who could order the sea to be still and it would obey. Jesus had gently asked them, "Why don't you believe? Why are you so afraid?" You see, He knew He was God's Son, and He could do impossible things. He wanted them to remember how much He loved them and how He would take care of them in all things. If Jesus could make the sea rest, He could surely make the people He loved feel safe.

Sometimes we may not understand why things happen the way they do, but don't forget, our Father knows everything, and He is in control. He is beside us all the time, and when we trust Him we can feel safe that He is taking care of us.

Questions:
    Could any of the disciples stop the storm?
    Did Jesus stop the storm?
    What are some things you are afraid of and want Jesus to
        help you with?

Prayer: Jesus, sometimes we are afraid, and we forget that You are with us and love us. Help us to remember You are taking care of us. Help us to trust You all the time. Amen.

A Lenten Activity: Think of someone who needs help. You may need to give food, clothes, or money. It may be taking care of your brother or sister or just giving your parents a big hug to let them know how much you love them and how much Jesus loves them too!

Calming the Storm
(ADULTS)

Scriptures: Psalm 124; Isaiah 43, 49:14-15; Matthew 8:23-27; Colossians 1:15-20

Devotion: You matter to God. When the storms of life unexpectedly overwhelm you with fear, you matter to God. When you think God is sleeping and He doesn't care, you matter to God. When you have followed God into the waters, and yet, the journey is anything but smooth sailing, you matter to God. You must believe this; otherwise, you will become hollow and disillusioned by the insurmountable waves. These are the times you cannot trust in a feeling but must lean solely on what Christ has done and has promised for us.

Scriptures tell us we live in a chaotic world. No one questions that all people, good or bad, experience physical or emotional pains. No one is promised smooth sailing, for this is not our Canaan. But Jesus reconciled the world to Himself by dying on the cross. Through His blood shed on the cross, He offers peace in every situation. As believers, we now have hope in something more powerful than any storm we will ever endure in this life, for He is the image of the invisible God. He also promises to be with us in the waters of life because of His great love for us. He climbs in our boats and is there throughout the entire journey. There are times when we feel God has lost control and that we're at the mercy of the winds of fate. It is then that many people become misdirected and put their confidence in other means of "salvation" such as knowledge, power, or money. We, as Christians, must hold on to our faith that Jesus is holding our lives together. He does not promise to save us from the storms, but if we have faith, He saves us in the storms.

In 1976, the Big Thompson River in Denver flooded. Eight carloads of Campus Crusade workers of Christ fled from an overnight Christian retreat. Six cars made it, but seven of the nine women in the other cars lost their lives. Ney Bailey, a survivor, knew she was capable of becoming bitter and cynical if she dwelled on the loss of her dear friends. Instead, she chose to focus on what God had given her instead of what was gone from her. Jesus Christ had said, "I am the Way, the Truth, and the Life." She chose to believe in this truth rather than on how she felt. These seven friends mattered to Christ and with her will, not her feelings, she found peace in Christ.

What have you been delivered from because of your faith in Christ? What do you want to be delivered from today? Think on these things. Resolve to follow Him and trust Him no matter what the cost.

Prayer: Lord, we don't know what storms we will confront today, but we trust You to be with us. In storm and in calm, keep us in Your perfect peace. Amen.

Abide in Me

Symbol: a vine with branches

Memory Verse: "I am the vine; ye are the branches. He that abideth in me, and I in him, the same bringeth much fruit: for without me you can do nothing." John 15:5 (KJV)

Songs to Sing:
   "This Is My Commandment" (John 15:12)
   "In My Life, Lord"
   "Trust and Obey"

Abide in Me
(CHILDREN)

Scriptures: John 15:1-17; Galatians 5:22-24

Devotion: Let's imagine we are walking with a farmer through his vegetable garden. He owns this garden and loves it very much. He will do everything he can to make it a good garden, so it will grow wonderful fruit. First, he digs in the ground to make it soft, and then he clears away any stones that could cause the plant not to grow. He finds the best vine and uses his hands to lovingly place it in the warm earth. Every day, he faithfully waters it, and the vine begins to grow. Soon, we see many branches have grown from the vine, and it looks so pretty and green! But wait! The farmer has some big scissors, and he's cutting his plant to pieces! When he finishes, all that is left is the vine with a few stems coming from it. It looks dead. Why do you think he does this? We ask him, and he tells us this is his garden, and whatever he wishes to do with it is his business and not ours. He then smiles and tells us to watch and wait.

After a few days, we see the little stems growing faster and stronger than ever. They are getting more water and food from the vine, and soon, little tomatoes are growing from the green leaves. At last the time has come to pick the fruit, and from the vine comes the plumpest, juiciest tomatoes of all the gardens. The wise farmer is very proud, and everyone praises him for his gardening.

Let's read this story in the Bible. God is the gardener of our lives and Jesus is the Vine. From Jesus, God wants us to grow and produce beautiful fruit. If we trust Christ and stay in Him, everyone will know we belong to God! Things may happen to us that we don't understand. Things may happen to us that we don't understand, but we know that God never turns away from us. God will be with us even when things hurt us. God loves us and wants us to put our trust in Christ. When we do, we will grow the fruit of the Spirit, which God says is love, joy, peace, patience, kindness, goodness, faithfulness, gentleness, and self-control. That is a lot of fruit, and God will be very happy!

Questions:
Who is our Gardener?
Who is the Vine?
What does God want us to do with the Vine?
What will happen if we stay a part of the Vine?

Prayer: Dear God, I want to show Your fruit to the world. I can't do this alone, and I need Jesus to help me. I know You love me and will take care of me when I stay close to You. Thank You. Amen.

A Lenten Activity: Visit a vegetable garden or plant a tomato plant. As it grows, remove the "suckers" or the stems that are not the fruit-bearing stems to show how the fruit gets its nourishment from the vine.

Abide in Me
(ADULTS)

Scriptures: Isaiah 5:1-2; Matthew 7:15-20; John 15:1-17; Romans 11:17-24; Galatians 5:22-24

Devotion: We all desire connection. Yet, too often, connection is broken because of betrayal and unbelief. The void experienced often results in self-doubt, anxiety, and depression. In John 15, however, Christ reveals the secret to having an intimate, sustaining relationship. The answer is abiding.

When we commit our lives to Him, God plants us with the Choicest Vine, His Son. The very life of Christ is rooted in our souls, and it is that root that supports us. Christ promises to remain faithfully true. Our part is to do the same. Abiding simply means to believe and stay with Him, and to receive His grace daily for our sustenance. Thus, the branch remains bound to the vine and receives nourishment for productive growth.

What happens when we experience this steadfast relationship with Christ? God prunes us to bear "much fruit." In marriage, couples vow to remain faithful, "for richer for poorer, for better for worse, in sickness and in health, till death do us part." If they endure the hardest of times, they are promised a productive life together. In vineyards, the gardener cuts back the branches so severely that they appear to be mere wooden stalks without life. Yet, greater nourishment is obtained and more fruit is produced. So it is during the pruning or the lowest moments of life that Christ becomes not only our Life Support but also our Friend. He understands all of our heartfelt tales of longings and pains. He comforts us, and it is then that anxiety turns into the fruit of peace, joy occurs out of depression, and hope emerges from hopelessness.

We must remember the fruit produced comes not from the works of our flesh but from the life within the Vine. We have love for others because the security gained from Christ's faithfulness empowers us to reach out to others. There are answered prayers because we want what God wants in our lives. We bear joy even in the midst of our trials, and that joy is complete.

Our lives are to be fruitful so that we may glorify God, and by our fruit people will recognize to whom we belong. Have you examined your own "fruit" lately? Is it good or bad— useful or wild? Are there areas in your life that need pruning away? If so, yield to the Gardener. Let Him do His work. Abide, grow, and bear.

Prayer: God, You are the Gardener of our lives. We thank You for giving us the Choicest of the vines. In Christ, you have given us Someone to abide with. Purge us and prune us, so that we will bring forth fruit pleasing to You. Water us with Your Love, so that we will be more conformed to the Vine. Amen.

Prepared for His Coming

Symbol: a lamp with oil

Memory Verse: "Be prepared, for you don't know what day your Lord is coming." Matthew 24:42 (TLB)

Songs to Sing:
   "Give Me Oil in My Lamp"
   "I Want to Be Ready"
   "Work, for the Night Is Coming"
   "I Know Where I'm Going"

Prepared for His Coming
(CHILDREN)

Scriptures: Matthew 24:42, 25:1-13

Devotion: What if someone invited you and your friends to go on a vacation with him? You'd be very excited, wouldn't you? But what if he came to pick you up and you weren't ready? Your suitcase was not packed because you had been watching TV and had fallen asleep. Your friend didn't have time to wait for you because the others would miss their plane. So, he left and went with those who were ready to go. That would make you very sad, wouldn't it?

Jesus was talking to His disciples about what would happen when He came back to earth to take them to heaven. Jesus liked to tell stories, and so He told them about ten women who were going to a wedding party. The women were very excited because they were going to go with the bridegroom. They didn't know, however, when the groom was going to come. Five of the women were very wise. They had put oil in jars and placed the jars beside their lamps. This way, if the groom came at night, they would be ready to go with him to the party. The other five, however, were foolish. They didn't think about what they might need, so they did nothing to get ready.

The women waited, but the groom did not come for a long time, and soon, they fell fast asleep. The night grew darker and darker, when suddenly, at midnight, there was a great shout! The groom was coming! The ten women jumped up and began to light their lamps. The wise women used the oil from their jars, but the foolish women did not have any oil. They ran to buy some more, but when they returned, it was too late. The party had already begun. The door was locked, and no one else could come in. The foolish women were very sad because they had not been ready! Only God knows when Jesus will come to take us to heaven. That's why Jesus wants us to always be ready.

Questions:
    What did the five wise women do to get ready for the
      groom?
    What happened to the foolish women?
    If Jesus came today, would you be ready for Him?

Prayer: Dear Jesus, we don't know when You are coming
again to take us to heaven. Help us obey, so whenever that
day is, we will be ready. We want You to be pleased when
You come for us. Keep our lights shining every day. Amen.

Prepared for His Coming
(ADULTS)

Scriptures: Matthew 24:36-44, 25:1-13; I Thessalonians 5:1-
15; 2 Timothy 1:8-10, 3:1-5; I Peter 1:13-15

Devotion: We have been pilgrims on a Lenten journey. Let
us pause and reflect on where we have been and what we
have learned. God's eternal plan for redemption of the
world is through Jesus Christ. We are taught that everyone
is responsible for his or her own spiritual condition. We
choose to either follow or reject His plan. If we trust Christ,
we are called to live Christ. Were we prepared for what He
has asked of us? Or, have we become complacent and foolish, thinking there is still time to get ready for Easter?

    Let us ponder where we are going and who is going with
us? Are we prepared to flee all evil desires and foolishness
of the world to pursue righteousness, faith, love, and peace?
Are we prepared to step into the unknown in faith? Are we
wise enough to remove any burdens that hinder our
progress along the way?

    We never know when our journey will end. Nor do we
know the day when Christ will come for His bride. If it were
today, would we be ready? Will we hear Him say to us,

"Well done, thou good and faithful servant," or the painful words, "I do not know you." We are called to examine our hearts for commitment. How we choose will determine our eternal destiny. Now is the time. There is no turning back.

Prayer: Jesus, You came so that we might have life. You have shown us the way to this abundant life if we are bold enough to follow Your teachings. We confess where we are weak. There are times we want to stop and give up. But You have taught that in You, we are made strong. Grant us the endurance to suffer whatever trials await us on our journey. Amen.

> If we died with him,
>   we will also live with him;
> if we endure,
>   we will also reign with him.
> If we disown him,
>   he will also disown us;
> if we are faithless,
>   he will remain faithful,
> for he cannot disown himself.

> II Timothy 2:11-13 (NIV)

Friendship and Forgiveness

Symbol: a mat for the paralytic man

Memory Verse: "Friend, your sins are forgiven." Luke 5:20 (NIV)

Songs to Sing:
   "Christ for the World We Sing"
   "Thank You Lord"
   "They'll Know We Are Christians by Our Love"

Friendship and Forgiveness
(CHILDREN)

Scripture: Luke 5:17-26

Devotion: Many people had come to hear Jesus speak. He was talking with them when suddenly He heard a noise above Him. He looked up and saw a hole being made in the ceiling of the room. Some men were lowering down a man who could not walk, and he was lying on a bed. They had tried to bring him to Jesus before, but there were too many people. They could not get through to Him, so they climbed the outside stairs to the top of the house and began to make a hole in the mud and straw roof. It took a lot of work, but they would not give up. They knew Jesus could heal their friend. As Jesus saw them lowering their friend in front of Him, He realized how much the men believed in Him. Because of their faith, Jesus turned to the man and told him that his sins were forgiven.

Immediately, the people began to question how He could forgive sins. No one could do that except God. Then Jesus did something amazing. He turned to the man and told him to get up and walk. Everyone was amazed that Jesus could forgive sins and also heal the sick. If the man had not had true friends to bring him to Jesus, he might never have been healed. Jesus wants us to be friends to those who are hurting and show them we care.

Do you need to be a friend to a sick person or someone who is lonely? You can visit and tell that person how much you love them. You can also help them know that Jesus cares. Bring your friends to Christ, just like the man's friends. Christ can forgive and take care of them forever.

Questions:
How did the men get their friend down to Jesus?
What was wrong with the man?
What did Jesus do?

Prayer: Dear Lord, I want to be a friend to others, and bring them to You. Help me to never give up telling others about Your love. Thank You that you heal not only our bodies but forgive our sins as well. Help us to believe, just like the man's friends, that You can do everything. Amen.

A Lenten Activity: Visit an elderly or sick person. Make a card or bring them something you have made that will remind them how much Jesus cares for them.

Friendship and Forgiveness
(ADULTS)

Scriptures: Micah 7:18, 19; Luke 5:17-26; Ephesians 1:4-8

Devotion: Jesus is teaching in a crowded room when a paralytic is lowered on a pallet in front of Him. He marvels at the faith of the paralytic's friends. A discussion arises about who can forgive sins besides God. Claiming the Son of Man has the same authority, Jesus turns to the paralytic and heals him. The crowd is amazed at the physical healing, but an even greater marvel is the healing of a soul!

Looking at how the Christian faith differs from the other major religions in the world, the answer is clear: forgiveness. It is the basis for our everyday living. Our assurance is in knowing that even though we will make mistakes and sin, the new life Christ proclaims enables us to live lives cleansed of sin. When we turn to Christ for the healing of our souls and humbly confess our sins, we are forgiven. Some argue that this forgiveness gives the believer freedom to sin more. The true believer, however, knowing the unconditional and freely given love of the Father, wants to live the same merciful behavior of the Lord before others. Jesus marveled at the faith of the paralytic's friends. Our faith affects others. We cannot make someone believe, but by our fruit they will know we are Christians and may seek the One we belong to.

Forgiveness involves restoring the person to wholeness. Once we have received forgiveness through God's love in Christ, we must forgive ourselves. Letting go of past failures, regrets, and fears brings peace within. This peace allows us to forgive others. Jesus teaches, "Forgive us our debts as we forgive our debtors." If we truly desire to follow in Christ's steps, we are to forgive not only our friends, but also our enemies and the unloving as well. The wholeness we have already received through God's love in Christ enables us to reach out and develop true friendships with others.

Prayer: Merciful God, forgive us our debt as we forgive our debtors. We are unworthy of this, but as You so freely give, we want to do the same. Work within us, as we love our neighbors, bringing all to healing and wholeness. Amen.

The Lily of the Valleys

Symbol: a lily

Memory Verse: "I am the rose of Sharon, and the lily of the valleys." Song of Solomon 2:1 (KJV)

Songs to Sing:
   "Everybody Ought to Know"
   "Lo, How a Rose E'er Blooming"
   "Pass It On"
   "Joyful, Joyful We Adore Thee"

The Lily of the Valleys
(CHILDREN)

Scripture: Song of Solomon 2:1; Matthew 6:28-30

Devotion: When we see an Easter lily, it reminds us of all the new life around us at springtime. This new life is what we have when we make Jesus our Lord. The lily's white color means purity. That means nothing is wrong with it. It is perfect, and that's the way Jesus is. He was without sin, pure and holy. When we see the lily, we remember Jesus, and what He did for us. The lily looks like a cup. Sometimes when we take communion at church, we drink from a cup. This cup reminds us that Jesus shed His blood for us so we could live.

The lily also reminds us of what happened to Jesus. Remember our devotion about the seed? In the winter, the lily looks as if it were dead. In fact, the bulb of the lily does die. But deep, in the soil, it begins to live again. The roots start to grow, and in the spring, the lily returns with all its glory. We should remember that even though it looked as if Jesus were dead, He would arise in all His glory.

Sometimes Jesus is called the Rose of Sharon. The rose means love. It is the most beautiful and fragile of all flowers, and yet it blooms to show how Christ loved us. When we see the rose, we remember this love.

All the flowers of spring remind us how God takes care of us. Jesus told a story about the lilies of the field. He reminded us that flowers don't work hard and don't need fine clothes because God has already made them beautiful. If God can take care of them, He will surely take care of us if we ask Him and do whatever He says.

Questions:
Who is the Lily of the Valleys?
When you see a flower what do you think of?
Will God take care of us?

Prayer: God, you are like a beautiful flower to us. We know You are love. We know You are perfect. We know You are there for us whenever we need You. Thank You for being so wonderful to us. Amen.

A Lenten Activity: Enjoy the beauty of God's nature today. Give a flower to someone and remind them that Jesus loves them.

The Lily of the Valleys
(ADULTS)

Scriptures: Song of Solomon 2:1; Matthew 6:28-34

Devotion: The blossoming flowers of springtime convey the eternal message of hope for mankind. Man has found within nature symbols of this hope through its rebirth and renewal, a reflection embodied in the risen Christ. In Matthew 6, we see how we need only to trust in the abundant care of God, for the One who paints the flowers is the same One who paints our lives. Christ, who is like the lilies of the field, is refreshing and beautiful to true believers. We are not to worry about what happens today or what could happen in the future but trust in Him as the flowers do for their sustenance and their joy. Christ wants us to turn to Him first for all help, to fill our thoughts with His desires, to take His character for His pattern in all things, and to serve Him and obey Him in everything. He will be like a rose, a flower constantly blooming to save us from sin and death and to share our every load. He will be extraordinary, like a lily among thorns!

What is really important to you? People, objects, goals, and other desires all compete for priority in your life. Any of these things can quickly bump God out if you don't actively choose to give Him first place in every area of your life. We should remember that clothes and money don't last. Praying for God's kingdom is more important than asking for bread or clothes. Don't let worries about your tomorrows affect your relationship with God today. Give Him first place, and you will find beauty and sweetness in Him. In return, once you have experienced the freshness of life that only God can give, you will want to pass it on to others. May His love be shed abroad as a field of lilies!

Prayer: Christ, our Lily of the Valley, You have taught us to trust You in all things. No matter what, You will make something beautiful out of our life if we will yield to Your plan. Help us to seek Your kingdom first, and then everything will be added unto us. We love You and give everything to You. Amen.

DAY TWENTY-SIX

A Gift of Love

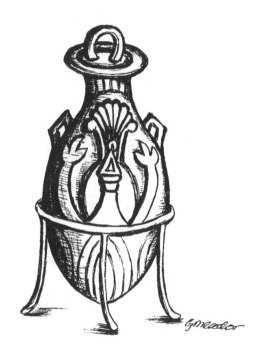

Symbol: a bottle of perfume

Memory Verse: "We love him, because he first loved us."
I John 4:19 (KJV)

Songs to Sing:
  "Father, I Adore You"
  "Jesus, I Just Want to Thank You"
  "Give of Your Best to the Master"

A Gift of Love
(CHILDREN)

Scriptures: John 12:1-7; I John 4:19

Devotion: One day, a big dinner was given for Jesus. His disciples and his closest friends were there, for they loved Him very much. A woman named Mary wanted to show Jesus just how much she loved Him, so she took a bottle of very precious perfume to give to Him. The perfume cost a lot of money, but she wanted to give the best that she had. She took the perfume, knelt down, and began pouring it on Jesus' feet! The fragrance of the perfume filled the entire room, and it smelled wonderful!

Mary had beautiful long hair and began to wipe His feet. But one of the disciples, named Judas, got very upset. He thought Mary had wasted the perfume, and the money should have been given to the poor. Jesus, however, was very pleased because He knew she was giving the most precious thing she had. He wanted her to use the perfume because she was trying to tell Him, "Thank You."

Jesus had been very kind to her. She believed that He was the Savior sent from God, and that He would take away her sins. She knew how much He loved her, and so she put the perfume on His feet to tell Him that she loved Him also. Jesus loves you, too. He loves you so much that He died for you to take away your sins. Have you thanked Him for this? If you do, He will be very pleased to see how much you love Him.

Questions:
Where did the woman put the perfume?
Was Jesus glad?
What can we give or do for Him to show Him we love Him?

Prayer: Jesus, when we think about how much You love us, we want to show our love for You. We want to give You the best that we have. We can never thank You enough for what

You have done for us, but we will serve You with our whole hearts. Amen.

A Lenten Activity: Give a gift of love. Take something that you have made or bought to a friend who means a lot to you—a pie, plant, or a small remembrance that has your love as a wrapping.

A Gift of Love
(ADULTS)

Scriptures: Mark 9:33-35; John 12:1-7; I John 4:19

Devotion: Jesus, the Son of God, knew He would become the Servant of God by dying to redeem the world. He had told His followers of his impending suffering and rejection. How fitting that Mary should anoint His body with expensive perfume in anticipation of His burial. Because of her servant attitude, God was working His plan in her life. This unique act was intended by God for the world to always remember Mary's gift of love.

There is a difference in choosing to serve and choosing to be a servant. When we choose to serve, we are still in control. We decide whom we will serve and when we will serve. Judas, upset by Mary's actions, had served Christ for the wrong motives. Judas thought he would have great status and a high position among the people in Christ's new political kingdom. Christ, however, knew that the busyness of serving as the group's treasurer had become a barrier for Judas to know Him personally.

In contrast, Mary had become a servant to Christ, completely devoted to Him and His spiritual kingdom. When we choose to be a servant, we surrender the right to decide who and when we will serve. We become available to sit and listen or to act in generous service. We also become vulnerable, believing no one is too good to stoop to the meanest of service whereby Christ may be honored. Jesus also knew Mary's heart, and He praised her for her thoughtful and worshipful action. She not only gave the best that she had, but with her own hands, poured the priceless ointment on Him.

The greatest sin is the rejection of Jesus Christ. What is Jesus to you? A name? A leader? Or your Master? Mary made her choice. She accepted Him as God's Son and man's Savior. She confessed Him before men by her actions, and she purposed to follow Him, even though it came at a cost. For her, it was a whole year's wage of perfumed oil. Are you willing to be a servant, no matter what the cost? Spend time with Him today, listen to His Word, and honor Him with all that you have.

Prayer: Master, we want to be involved in helping and serving. Yet, we must listen to Your Word and learn what you desire of us. Give us a servant's heart. We pour on You the ointment of our best affections. We give you our all. Amen.

DAY TWENTY-SEVEN

Jesus, the Man of Prayer

Symbols: hands in prayer

Memory Verse: "Father, if you are willing, take this cup from me; yet not my will, but yours be done." Luke 22:42 (NIV)

Songs to Sing:
   "I Stand Amazed in the Presence"
   "Where He Leads Me"
   "More Love to Thee, O Christ"
   "In the Garden"

Jesus, the Man of Prayer
(CHILDREN)

Scriptures: Luke 22:39-48

Devotion: Jesus loved to talk to His Father. Sometimes He would get up early in the morning to pray. Sometimes He would stay up late at night, but He would always go to God about everything. One night Jesus went into a garden to pray. He was very sad. He knew why He had come to earth. He had left His throne in heaven to give up His life, so all the world could be saved. He also knew that some men were going to come and take Him away. They would nail Him to a cross. Jesus did not want to die like this. He needed to talk to His Father, so He began to pray and told God how He was feeling.

Jesus could have called the angels to protect Him, but He loved His Father so much and loves us so much that He didn't do that. Instead, He prayed for God to make Him strong, and God sent an angel to help Him. He wanted to do what God wanted and not what He wanted.

Jesus is still praying for us. He knows just what we need. He knows when we want to do wrong, and He is always asking His Father to keep us from sin. Even though He's in heaven, He knows everything we do, and He prays that we will love one another.

Jesus also wants us to talk to Him and tell Him all about ourselves. He wants us to tell Him what we like or don't like and what we are doing. He wants us to tell Him when we are happy or sad. He wants us to tell Him everything.

Questions:
Was Jesus happy or sad in the garden?
What did Jesus know was going to happen to Him?
What is He doing for us right now?

Prayer: Jesus, keep on praying for us. We will try to be good. Thank You that we can come and talk to You about anything that happens to us. We pray in Your name. Amen.

A Lenten Activity: Make pretzels (see Appendix). It is thought that originally pretzels were made by monks about A.D. 610 to resemble arms crossed in prayer. These little breads were called "little arms" or "bracellae." Hence we have the word pretzel today!

Jesus, the Man of Prayer
(ADULTS)

Scriptures: Isaiah 53:3; Luke 22:39-46; Philippians 2: 5-8, 4:6; Hebrews 5:7

Devotion: All of us have experienced times of heartache and overwhelming sorrow. The pressures of life can weigh us down to the point of exhaustion, fear, and failure. Jesus, the "man of sorrows," understands these times of suffering. He found His answers through prayer, and He commands us to do the same.

Jesus came to the Garden of Gethsemane with real needs. Scriptures tell us that he was deeply distressed and troubled, and His sweat was like drops of blood falling to the ground. Medical research tells us that under great emotional stress, tiny capillaries in the sweat glands can break, causing the phenomenon of hematidrosis, or bloody sweat. Whether the scripture is a comparison to blood or actual blood is irrelevant. What we do see in this garden is immense torment and pain beyond human comprehension. We see a man struggling with fear, wrestling with commitments, and yearning for relief. God was never more human than at this hour.

The easy part of prayer is yielding to God when we don't know the answer. It becomes difficult when we clearly know God's answer, yet we do not want to follow it. Prayer is honestly laying before God the desires and burdens of our hearts. It is also centering our attention away from ourselves toward God, so we can absorb the truths by which He wants us to live. This was the war fought in the garden that night—the war of wills. Jesus' will was for the bitter cup to pass from Him. The Father's will was total submission from His Son. Jesus came into the garden troubled, confused, and struggling with the desires of a human heart. He needed to talk with His Father. The flesh was strong, but in the end, His desire to glorify the Father was stronger. By submitting, He was strengthened. He left the garden resolved to endure the worst forms of human suffering for you and me.

What are you struggling with at this exact moment? Is it an adulterous affair, an unhealthy relationship, or an addictive lifestyle? Is it a job decision, physical infirmity, or financial uncertainty? It could be guilt, grief, family strife—the topics are endless. The moment any of these anxious thoughts invade your mind, go to God in prayer, just as Jesus did. Surrender to His will, and by following it, you will find ultimate peace.

Prayer: There is a battle going on inside us. Give us the strength not to fall into temptation. Help us to have a servant mind, a mind that puts You above everything else. We bring our concerns and lay them at your feet. Teach us how to learn from our sufferings lest they make us bitter. Lord, it comforts us to know we can pray in Your name, the One who completely identifies with us in everything. Amen.

Devotion or Denial

Symbol: a rooster

Memory Verse: "I am not ashamed of the gospel of Christ."
Romans 1:16 (KJV)

Songs to Sing:
   "I'll Tell the World That I'm a Christian"
   "Stand Up, Stand Up for Jesus"
   "Are You Able, Said the Master"

Devotion or Denial
(CHILDREN)

Scriptures: Psalm 59:16; Luke 22:31-34, 54-63

Devotion: "I won't!" cries Peter to the Lord. "I won't leave you. In fact, I am ready to die for you." Jesus had just told His disciples that all of them would leave Him that night, like sheep scattering from their shepherd. Proud Peter knew he would never do that to his friend. He was always ready to speak out and act bravely for his master, and he would fight to his death if anyone else went against him. But Jesus knew Peter better than Peter knew himself. He said, "Peter, let me tell you something. Between now and tomorrow morning when the rooster crows, you will deny Me three times, saying that you don't even know Me."

Do you know what the word "deny" means? It means to say something is not true or that you don't believe in it. Jesus knew that before the evening ended, brave Peter would lie. The thought of this must have hurt Jesus very much, but do you know what He did? He began to pray for Peter, so that when he did deny Him, he would be sorry and would come back to Him.

That night, Jesus was arrested and taken to the high priest's home. Peter followed, but at a distance. Some people were warming themselves by a fire in the courtyard, and Peter sat with them. A young girl noticed him and said he was a disciple. Peter said, "No." Why do you think he did this? Peter was ashamed to tell the truth because he didn't want to be laughed at, and he was afraid the people would hurt him if they knew he was Jesus' friend. Peter said, "No" again and again, and when the next morning began with the rooster's crow, Peter had denied Jesus three times. Hearing the rooster, Peter looked up and saw Jesus looking at him. It was a look that broke Peter's heart. With this look, Peter remembered what he had done to Jesus. He began to cry because he had denied the friend he loved so much.

Whenever someone asks you if Jesus is your friend, He wants you to say yes. He does not want you to be afraid to tell others about Him. Will you be His friend, or will you deny Him?

Questions:
Was Jesus a friend of Peter?
What did Peter tell the young girl?
Should you be afraid to say Jesus is your friend?

Prayer: Dear Jesus, as I begin each day, may I remember the rooster's crow to be loyal to You. You are my friend, and I don't won't to be afraid to tell others how much I love You. Help me to stand up for You. Amen.

Devotion or Denial
(ADULTS)

Scriptures: Psalm 59:16; Luke 22:31-34, 54-63; Romans 7:19, 8:5, 12:2-3; Revelation 3:8

Devotion: In his shameful denial of Christ, Peter ironically portrays the human condition of many believers today. Peter had a preconceived idea of what the Christian life really was. He had never grasped the reality that though the spirit is willing, the flesh is weak. And yet, positive that he could handle any situation and Satan had no tricks he could not evade, Peter walked in self-confidence and pride, boasting boldly of his undying devotion and love for Jesus. Peter could not see that pride would go before his fall. Jesus had warned him of this, but Peter's self-righteousness boasted in his own strength and stability. Jesus knew Peter had to learn about himself and the true nature of his own heart before he could truly become a usable vessel for Christ.

The moment he vowed would never come had arrived,

and Peter heard himself deny the Lord he loved not once, but three times. Immediately a cock crowed, and his eyes met the gaze of Jesus. Waves of memories crushed Peter into a broken and humiliated man. The fall he had expected of everyone else had become his! All his self-confidence, pride, and self-sufficiency spilled out in bitter tears. He could not rest in his promise of what he would or wouldn't do. He could not turn to others, for they had also deserted Christ. The breaking point had come for Peter, and the result was denial.

What are our breaking points? What are the ways we disown Jesus? What are the areas in our lives where we are prideful and arrogant? Just as Peter, in our enthusiasm, it is easy to make promises, but God knows the extent of our commitment. He knows what pride and piety can do to a life. He also knows that when our defenses are down, we become vulnerable. It is then that we must rest, not in our own strength, but in the acceptance of God through the sacrificial death of Christ.

Peter became a better man in spite of his sin. Because of his failures, Peter learned that the love Jesus gave him was not because of anything he earned or deserved. We too can know that though our religion, promises, and performances may fail, Jesus' love never fails. In spite of ourselves, Jesus' love never changes.

Prayer: Merciful Father, we have offended You with our everyday denials. Have mercy upon us as we confess our faults. Teach us to greet each new day with a faith so consuming that we will witness to the truth in Christ in every situation that confronts us. Help us to order our lives that we will never forsake you. Amen.

The Betrayer

Symbol: thirty pieces of silver

Memory Verse: "You were bought at a price."
I Corinthians 7:23 (NIV)

Songs to Sing:
  "Jesus Paid It All"
  "O How He Loves You and Me"
  "Jesus Loves Even Me"

The Betrayer
(CHILDREN)

Scriptures: Matthew 26:14-16, 20-25, 47-50, 27:3-5; I Corinthians 7:23a

Devotion: Do you know who Judas Iscariot was? He was one of Jesus' disciples, and he took care of the money. He loved money. In fact, he loved it so much that he would steal some of it when Jesus and the other disciples weren't looking. He would just help himself whenever he wanted some. He pretended to be Jesus' friend, but he was really only looking out for himself.

At first, Judas thought Jesus was going to be a king on this earth, and Judas would become very famous. But Jesus kept talking about how His kingdom was not of this earth. He kept saying how He was going to die, and this was not what Judas wanted to hear. So, Judas went to some bad men and told them he would help them catch Jesus if they would give him money. The men gave Judas 30 pieces of silver, and Judas began his evil plan.

On the night before He was killed, Jesus ate supper with Judas and the disciples. He loved Judas and was willing to share His bread and wine with him. But Judas didn't care how Jesus felt. He was going to do what he wanted to do. Later that night Jesus went to a garden. Judas knew that Jesus usually spent time praying there, so he led the bad men to Jesus. He ran to Him and kissed Him on the cheek. This was the sign to show the soldiers which one was Jesus. Jesus did not run away but simply looked at Judas and said, "Friend, do what you came for." The men arrested Jesus, and all the disciples ran away.

Even though he had gotten his money, Judas was not happy. He kept remembering how Jesus had called him, "Friend." Finally, he went again to the men and asked them to take back the money, but the men would not take it. They knew Jesus had done nothing wrong, but they still wanted to kill Him. Brokenhearted, Judas threw the money on the floor and ran out. He was so sad that he had been unfaithful, and instead of asking Jesus to forgive him, he killed himself.

Questions:
   Who was the man who led the bad people to Jesus?
   Why did Judas betray Jesus?
   Why do you think Judas killed himself?

Prayer: Lord, it is so sad to think about how Judas killed himself. Judas was sad because he was unfaithful. Help us to not love anything more than You, and may we be faithful to You in everything. Thank You for letting us be Your friend even when we do things You are not happy about. Amen.

A Lenten Activity: Instead of coins, look at a bag full of jelly beans. Read "The Jelly Bean Prayer" (see Appendix).

The Betrayer
(ADULTS)

Scriptures: Matthew 26:14-25, 47-50, 27:3-10; Romans 8:24; I Corinthians 7:23; I Peter 1:18-19; James 2:18-19

Devotion: A famous scene from an award-winning movie shows a young boy confiding to his psychologist, "There are dead people walking around who don't even know they're dead." Such was the case of Judas Iscariot. From the outside, he probably was no different from the other disciples. He looked like a branch attached to the vine. In reality, he was dead and fruitless, never having the life of Christ in him.

Judas yearned for "the kingdom of God" to come. He thought it would be an earthly kingdom, replacing the tyrannical rule of the Romans. He looked to Jesus to be the savior, but only as a political leader who would revolutionize the world. When it became apparent that Jesus' ways were not his ways, Judas committed one of the most heinous acts ever. He bargained with the chief priests for the betrayal of his friend, and Jesus was bought with a price of thirty silver coins.

In the book of James, we are warned to not confuse mere intellectual assent with true faith. After all, even demons know who Jesus is, but they don't obey Him. We may acknowledge Jesus as Lord of our lives but live otherwise, seeking money, power, and our own desires. We may, in actuality, be separated from the only One who gives us life and not even know it. True faith involves a commitment of our whole selves to God's way and not our way. In the end, Judas was overwhelmed with remorse. The money or power did not matter anymore. If Judas had turned to the Savior, he would have found forgiveness. Instead, he still did not understand the way of Christ and how even the worst of sinners can find the kingdom of God.

The name "Iscariot" is suggested to mean "liar." Are we, like Judas, living a lie when it comes to our salvation? Are we alive or dead in Christ? Let us examine what master we are serving, and forsaking all others, choose to believe and trust in Jesus, our Savior and Friend.

Prayer: Dear Jesus, we are all guilty of sin. The evidence is clear. We know the sentence should be death, but because of Your great love, You took our punishment upon Yourself. By Your death, we are free. The penalty has been paid in full. Forgive us when we can't see the areas of our lives that need to be brought under Your control. Thank You for calling us "Friend," even though we are unworthy. Help us revolutionize the world by following Your rule of loving our enemies. Amen.

The Scourging of Jesus

Symbol: a flagellum or whip

Memory Verse: "By his wounds you have been healed."
1 Peter 2:24 (NIV)

Songs to Sing:
  "Wounded for Me"
  "And Can It Be That I Should Boast"
  "When I Survey the Wondrous Cross"

The Scourging of Jesus
(CHILDREN)

Scriptures: John 19:1; I Peter 2:21-24

Devotion: After the soldiers had arrested him, Jesus was taken to three different men. The last man they took Him to was a man by the name of Pilate. He asked Jesus if He was a king. Jesus told him that His kingdom was not on earth and that He always told the truth. Pilate did not want Jesus to be killed, but he didn't want the people to be mad. So, he decided to punish Jesus instead by whipping Him.

He told a soldier to take a whip that had three straps. The whip had pieces of bone, glass, and metal in the strap, so it would cut the person that it touched. This was a very mean thing to do, wasn't it? Jesus had done nothing wrong, and yet He was going to be whipped.

The soldiers took Jesus' shirt off, so He could be hurt. They hit Him thirty-nine times, and every time the whip touched Him, a deep cut was made in His back. Blood came out, and Jesus was in a lot of pain. He could have been mean back to the bad people, but He wasn't. He let them hurt Him because this was God's plan. Jesus knew He would have to be beaten and die on the cross. After they whipped Him, Pilate took Jesus out to the people again and asked them what to do with Him. The people told Pilate to kill Jesus, and so He was taken to the cross to die.

Jesus was very sad and He hurt so much, but because He loved us, He died for us. He never wants us to hurt from the bad things we do. That's why He was willing to be hit and killed. Let's say our memory verse together, and remember He did this for us (I Peter 2:24).

Questions:
What did the soldier do to Jesus?
Did it hurt Jesus?
Did Jesus hurt the bad people?

Prayer: Jesus, it makes us so sad when we think about what they did to You. We know You let them do it because You love us and want us to be with You. Thank You for suffering for us. Help us to never be mean to anyone like the soldiers were to You. We love You. Amen.

The Scourging of Jesus
(ADULTS)

Scriptures: Matthew 25:40; John 12:23-28; I Peter 2:21-24, 5:5-11; 2 Timothy 4:5

Devotion: One of the most convicting and heart wrenching scenes in the musical *Jesus Christ Superstar* is the scourging of Jesus. No words are sung, and only one simple motif is heard playing continuously. Yet, as every sound of the 39 lashes intensifies, the horrible and torturous pain Jesus endured for each of us penetrates into the heart of the listener.

Scourging was done with a triple-ended whip called a flagellum. The whip had bits of bone, metal, or glass in the ends of its straps. The offender was stripped. His arms and legs were then tied to rings beside a low pillar, so the body's back could be stretched and exposed to the executioner's blows. The strokes were laid on with full force. As the flogging continued, the lacerations would tear into the underlying skeletal muscles producing deep bloody holes. The thirty-nine lashes would penetrate deeper into the torn flesh until the very bones of the victim could be seen. This was what happened to Jesus. He underwent the punishment of the whip, so we might be healed.

The torture of Jesus doesn't make sense to us. If He had to die for our salvation, couldn't it have been a painless and easy death? Did He have to be beaten, spit upon, mocked, scourged, pierced, and nailed to a cross? Jesus tells us it was

necessary. If He had not endured the worst of human torture, many would not claim the resurrection and His power
over death. Scourging was intense and sometimes fatal.
Jesus' physical condition was critical even to the point of
death before the actual crucifixion. The resurrection was a
miracle because no human could have endured what He did
and come back to life. His resurrection proves He is God
and because He is God, Jesus can give the same eternal life
to all who believe in Him.

Jesus also endured these things, so we could learn how to
bear the hardships in our lives. We are called to obey the
Father and glorify Him in all our sufferings. Hate and retal-
iation should never be used to wound those who mistreat
us. If we lash out at anyone, we are making another stripe
in His body.

Prayer: Jesus, my heart aches when I think of what they did
to You. Yet, every time I lash out and hurt my brother, I am
wounding You. I know every ugly deed is but another lash
in Your back. Forgive me of this, and help me to follow Your
example when others treat me unkindly in my sufferings.
Amen.

The Crown of Thorns

Symbol: a crown of thorns

Memory Verse: "He was oppressed, and he was afflicted, yet he opened not his mouth." Isaiah 53:7 (KJV)

Songs to Sing:
  "My Jesus, I Love Thee"
  "O Sacred Head Now Wounded"
  "Jesus Is All the World to Me"

The Crown of Thorns
(CHILDREN)

Scriptures: Isaiah 53:7; Matthew 27:27-31

Devotion: Have you ever had someone make fun of you? Even if you did nothing wrong, and they were still mean to you, it hurt, didn't it? What do you do when someone is ugly to you? There is a story in the Bible about what Jesus did when He was laughed at.

Remember how some people didn't like Jesus, so they took Him to Pilate? Pilate knew that these people were just jealous and wanted to be mean to Jesus. He turned to a big crowd that had gathered, and he told them that Jesus had done nothing wrong. But the angry people cried, "Crucify Him," and Pilate followed the crowd. He gave Jesus to the soldiers. Let's read the story. It will hurt you to hear what happened, but remember it hurt Jesus even more (Matthew).

The soldiers placed a crown on Jesus' head and put a robe on Him. This usually meant that honor was being given to a hero. But the soldiers weren't doing this. Instead, they were making fun of Jesus by dressing Him up like a king. In place of a royal crown, they made a crown of thorns from a thorny plant and put it on Him. They walked around Him saying mean things to Him. They hit him again and again on his head, and soon, blood ran down His face from the thorns. They put a king's staff in His hand and knelt down to bow to Him, but instead of worshipping Him, they laughed at Him. This hurt Jesus very much, but do you know what He did?

He never said a word. He was in great pain, and He wanted to run away and hide, but He didn't. He still loved the soldiers and forgave them because they did not know He was God's Son. He did this for you and me, too. He was willing to be hit and laughed at, so He could be King of our hearts. Now next time, when someone makes fun of you, remember Jesus went through the same pain. He will be there with you and will help you with your hurt.

Questions:
What did the soldiers do to Jesus?
What did Jesus do?
Is Jesus king of your heart?

Prayer: Dear Lord, You are our King. Whenever someone makes fun of us, help us remember the crown of thorns. May we never make fun of anyone because we know how much it hurts. Amen.

A Lenten Activity: A thorn taken from a rose may show a child some of the pain Jesus went through. If available, show the cacti plant called the Crown of Thorns. It is covered with stout spines resembling thorns and small bright scarlet flowers, signifying the blood of Christ.

A Crown of Thorns
(ADULTS)

Scriptures: Isaiah 53:7; Matthew 5:11-12, 27:11-31

Devotion: The crown of thorns is a symbol of Christ's suffering and humiliation. At the time of Christ's life, heroes were crowned with a wreath of laurel leaves. Jesus' followers called Him the "King of the Jews," so the soldiers made a crown of thorns to mock Him. They pierced His brow, spit upon Him, and cursed Him for hours. Although He was God, Jesus endured the cruel mocking without complaining. This He did for our sake.

Physical abuse may be far removed from some people, yet many of us have experienced some form of verbal abuse. There are many times that we have our feelings hurt, whether it be in a word of disapproval from an employer or co-worker, a quick angry reaction from a loved one, or ugly gossip in a telephone call. Hurting words cut us to the deepest part of our emotions, leaving us with feelings of loneliness, inadequacy, and rejection. Our innate reaction is self-protection and revenge, and so we retaliate with words and looks that cover our fears of weakness. It's very hard to "turn the other cheek" when one feels like running away or fighting back, yet Christ lived the words He taught by enduring the worst taunting and abuse ever given. His reaction was not natural but supernatural. He was faithful to the path He had chosen to follow, suffering for our sakes and bearing our sins to make us acceptable to God. Are we willing to be faithful to His radical teachings and responses, to suffer for Him and others when the result could be pain and rejection? Let us stand with Christ, forgiving those who wrongfully abuse us, and work in peace for all.

Prayer: Lord and King, we pray for those who persecute us. Help us to work for peace in a world that is full of violence and hate. Open our eyes that we may see the needs of others, and that we may never be afraid to defend any who are wrongfully abused. By our compassion, use us to bring them to You. Give us all the assurance of Your presence in times of rejection and mourning. Come, our King, sit upon the throne of our hearts and reign forever. Amen.

Christ, Our King

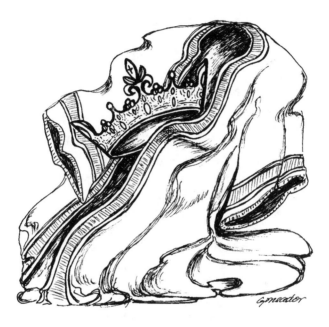

Symbol: a robe and crown

Memory Verse: "Worthy is the Lamb that was slain to receive power, and riches, and wisdom, and strength, and honor, and glory, and blessing." Revelation 5:12 (KJV)

Songs to Sing:
  "We Will Glorify"
  "My Eternal King"
  "Crown Him with Many Crowns"
  "What Child Is This"

Christ, Our King
(CHILDREN)

Scriptures: John 18:33–19:6; Revelation 5:11-14, 14:14, 19:16

Devotion: Do you remember how the soldiers were mean to Jesus before they crucified Him? They put a purple robe on Him and made a crown of thorns for his head. They spit on Him and laughed at Him saying, "Hail, King of the Jews." This hurt Jesus, but He let them do this because He loved us very much.

One of the rulers named Pilate asked Jesus if He really was a king, and Jesus told him it was true. This was why he had come into the world as a little baby. Jesus told the people standing around that if they listened to Him and put Him as their King, everyone could be part of His heavenly kingdom. But no one would listen to Jesus, and instead of worshipping Him, they killed Him!

We know the story doesn't end here. We know that Jesus died, and the devil wanted Him to stay in the grave. The devil wanted everyone to die, but Jesus wanted everyone to live. When Jesus rose from the grave, He beat the devil, and now He is our victorious King in heaven. Let's read our scriptures in Revelation. One day, He will come for us. We will see him in the sky, and He will be seated on a glorious throne in a white cloud. On His head will be a crown, but it will not be a crown of thorns. It will be a crown of gold, and on His robe will be His name: KING OF KINGS AND LORD OF LORDS. Everyone who loves the King of Kings will be singing praises to Him. They will be wearing white robes and on their heads will be crowns, too. Jesus will reign as King forever! Won't this be wonderful?

Questions:

Is Jesus the King?

Where is Jesus now?

What will He be wearing when He comes again?

Prayer: Jesus, You are our King. Thank You for leaving Your throne in heaven and coming to the earth. Thank You for dying on the cross. Thank You for beating sin so we could live forever! We praise you and honor You. Amen.

Christ, Our King
(ADULTS)

Scriptures: John 18:33–19:6; II Timothy 4:7-8; James 1:12; Hebrews 2:9; Revelation 5:11-14, 6:2 and 11, 14:14, 19:11-16

Devotion: "What is Truth?" asked by Pilate and many of us about Jesus. Was He just a good man, a prophet equal to Moses and Elijah, or truly the King above all kings? Jesus Christ said, "I am the Alpha and the Omega, . . . who is, and who was, and who is to come, the Almighty" (Revelation 1:8 NIV). To discover if this is truth, we must go to the scriptures, read the evidence, and determine the verdict of this man we call Jesus.

We need to see Christ for who He is. "In the beginning was the Word, and the Word was with God, and the Word was God. He was with God in the beginning. Through him all things were made; without him nothing was made that has been made. In him was life, and that life was the light of men" (John 1:1-4 NIV). "I am the way, the truth, and the life. No one comes to the Father except through me" (John 14:6 NIV). "You are a king, then!" said Pilate. Jesus answered, "You are right in saying I am a king. In fact, for this reason I was born, and for this I came into the world, to testify to the truth. Everyone on the side of truth listens to me"(John 18:37 NIV).

We need to see Christ for what He has done. "The Word became flesh and made his dwelling among us. We have seen his glory, the glory of the One and Only, who came from the Father, full of grace and truth" (John 1:14 NIV).

"But God demonstrates his own love for us in this: While we were still sinners, Christ died for us"(Romans 5:8 NIV). "For God was pleased to have all his fullness dwell in him, and through him to reconcile to himself all things, whether things on earth or things in heaven, by making peace through his blood, shed on the cross" (Colossians 1:19-20 NIV).

We need to see Christ for who is to come. "They will make war against the Lamb, but the Lamb will overcome them because he is Lord of lords and King of kings—and with him will be his called, chosen and faithful followers" (Revelation 17:14 NIV). "Let us rejoice and be glad and give him glory! For the wedding of the Lamb has come, and his bride has made herself ready . . . 'Blessed are those who are invited to the wedding supper of the Lamb!' And he added, 'These are the true words of God'" (Revelation 19:7, 9 NIV).

Read the book of John. Examine the truths. Either you believe all or nothing. The choice is yours.

Prayer: Lord, You have told us that unless we are born again, we will not see the kingdom of God. We profess our belief that you are King above all kings. Help us have no others ruling in our lives. We thank You that You have chosen us to be saved through Your sanctifying work of the Spirit. We believe in Your truth. Amen.

The Ride into Jerusalem

Symbol: a donkey

Memory Verses: "See, your king comes to you, gentle and riding on a donkey." Matthew 21:5 (NIV)

"Come to me, all you who are weary and burdened, and I will give you rest. Take my yoke upon you and learn from me, for I am gentle and humble in heart, and you will find rest for your souls. For my yoke is easy and my burden is light." Matthew 11:28-29 (NIV)

Songs to Sing:
  "Hosanna, Loud Hosanna"
  "What a Friend We Have in Jesus"
  "Be Still, My Soul"

The Ride into Jerusalem
(CHILDREN)

Scriptures: Mark 11:1-7; Zechariah 9:9

Devotion: When Jesus was alive on earth, the Roman government treated the people of Israel very badly. Many of the Israelites remembered a promise that had been told to them. It was about a king who would come one day to rescue the people from their burdens. The people heard about the good things Jesus had done. They believed He was this king who would destroy the Romans and set up a wonderful kingdom for them. When they heard he was coming to Jerusalem, they prepared for His grand entrance as a great king. But Jesus did not come to fight wars and to hurt people. He was not asking for power and glory on earth. He wanted to have a different kind of kingdom where the king would be a servant to the people. In return, the people would treat each other kindly.

Jesus told two of His disciples to go into the city. There they would find a donkey that had never been ridden on. The disciples must have thought that this was a strange animal for a king, but they did what Jesus asked them to do. Sure enough, there was a donkey right where Jesus had told them it would be. The disciples borrowed the donkey and brought him back to Jesus. They put their coats on the donkey's back, and Jesus sat on the donkey. He chose to ride a donkey into Jerusalem to show He was not a king of war, but a king of peace.

Just as Jesus Christ our King entered Jerusalem, He can enter our hearts as king if we let Him. He will not fight His way into our lives, but He will come in to give us peace forever. He will also help us serve others. Let's enter His kingdom by asking Him to come into our hearts.

Questions:
What did Jesus ask His disciples to do?
Did they obey Him?
What kind of king is Jesus?

Prayer: Lord, enter our hearts and be the king. When You tell us to do something, may we obey you, just like the disciples did. And help us to be kind to people just as You are kind. Amen.

A Lenten Activity: Take a trip to the zoo and see a donkey. Legend says that the donkey was one color before it carried Christ into Jerusalem. Today, the sign of the cross can clearly be seen on the donkey's back, a reminder of the humble King who once rode the lowly beast.

The Ride into Jerusalem
(ADULTS)

Scriptures: Psalm 24:7-10; Zechariah 9:9; Mark 11:1-7

Devotion: Beasts of burdens—donkeys or the human race?

Donkeys were known as creatures of great stamina. They were valued not only as riding animals by the Hebrews, common and influential alike, but also as carriers of great burdens such as grains and provisions. The small but sturdy backs would carry huge loads for long journeys until their masters saw fit to relieve them.

Throughout life, burdens have also been imposed on humans. In the Old Testament, we find the Israelites being burdened by the Egyptians in servitude, and then there was the burden of diligently following the 613 laws that God had given them through Moses. The Lord Himself carried a burden for Israel as He wept when approaching Jerusalem. He knew they had not realized what would bring them real peace, and His heart ached for them.

And so begins the last week of Christ's life. The people are looking to Christ to loose the burdens of injustice, to untie the cords of the yoke, and to set them free. The people correctly see Him as a king but not the kind of king they understand. He is a king who has no place to lay His head, a king who chooses to enter His kingdom without heralds or an impressive army but on the back of a borrowed beast. Christ knows His purpose. He comes, not "to be served, but to serve, and to give his life as a ransom for many" (Mark 10:45 NIV). He is a king who asks his followers to take upon them His burden, a burden of humility and servitude. In so doing, the believer will experience a freedom and rest for the soul that only his Master can give.

Today, we are still looking to Christ to free us from the trials and tribulations of life. But there is no promise of a life without burdens. He does, however, promise to help carry those burdens. When we take on the yoke of Christ, we have joy knowing that He is with us, showing us how to live this journey of life. Let us, being redeemed, follow His example and go forth to serve.

Prayer: Our sins and griefs are heavy, Christ, and we are weak and discouraged. We know You have promised to bear those burdens if we only carry them to You. Guide us in the way You want us to go through life, and give us the humility to take our burdens to Your cross and to leave them there.

Hosanna! The King Cometh

Symbol: palm branches

Memory Verses: "The crowds that went ahead of him and those that followed shouted, 'Hosanna to the Son of David! Blessed is he who comes in the name of the Lord! Hosanna in the highest!'" Matthew 21:9 (NIV)

"The Son of Man did not come to be served, but to serve, and to give his life as a ransom for many." Mark 10:45 (NIV)

Songs to Sing:
   "All Glory, Laud, and Honor"
   "Tell Me the Stories of Jesus"
   "Alleluia"

Hosanna! The King Cometh
(CHILDREN)

Scriptures: Matthew 21:8-11; Revelation 7:9-10

Devotion: Do you know why we call today Palm Sunday? Let's read in Matthew about this very special day.

Do you remember what Passover was about? It was Passover week, and the Jews from all over the Roman world were in Jerusalem to celebrate the holiday. The streets were crowded and on this day, the air was filled with excitement as Jesus rode into Jerusalem on a donkey. The people thought Jesus would crown himself king of Israel when He arrived. They wanted Jesus to be king because He had been kind to them and had done many miracles. Many people took off their coats and put them on the ground for Jesus to ride over. Others cut down branches from the trees and made a path for Him. The people shouted in loud voices "Hosanna," and they began to praise God joyfully for all the miracles He had done. Some wanted them to be quiet, but Jesus told them that even if there was silence, the stones would speak up and praise God. You can see why everyone was happy, can't you? The people praised God that Jesus, their king, had come. They did not know that Jesus would soon be killed.

Jesus is in heaven now. But one day He will come back again and people will wave branches to praise Him as the victorious king. He will take all His people who love Him to live in heaven with Him. We have a lot to praise Him for, don't we? Let's do that right now.

Questions:
Were the people happy?
What did they put down on the road for Jesus to ride over?
Why did they do this?
Can you think of some things we should praise God for?

Prayer: (Have children think of two things to praise God for. Have them thank Him in prayer.) We praise You, God, just like the people did on Palm Sunday. Thank You for sending us Jesus to be our king. Thank you for all the other things You have done for us. Amen.

Hosanna! The King Cometh
(ADULTS)

Scriptures: Psalms 24:7-10, 118:19-29; Matthew 21:8-11; Mark 10:32-34, 43-45; Revelation 7:9-10, 19:11-16

Devotion: As Passion Week begins, it is important for us to remember the events that led up to his last hours. One such event was when Jesus told the Pharisees He would continue His journey to Jerusalem. He knew He would face death, but He did not veer from His course. He had "not come to be served, but to serve, and to give his life as a ransom for many" (Mark 10:45 NIV). The chorus of a popular song has Jesus saying to God, "I will go the distance. I will go that far. I will go the distance to get them where you are."

It was no wonder that the people lined the streets that day to praise Him, placing their robes and palm branches in His path. The palm was a symbol of prosperity and victory, and they were sure liberation was at hand. This Jesus would lead them to victory over their oppressors and the poverty they were enduring. He would restore the nation to its former glory and establish his kingdom forever. But Jesus wanted to be King of their lives, not of their country, and this was where their adoration became short-lived and without commitment. The shouts of "Hosanna" turned to "Crucify Him" only a few days later.

Too often, we, as human beings, change our loyalties when the going gets tough. Our vision of what God has called us to be and to do dims. The pressures and the decisions we have made seem to blow up in our faces, so we "throw in the towel." We do not finish the course we have chosen and begin to doubt our allegiance to God. In these times, we fail to remember that our Guide is constant, dependable, and above all, faithful and just. He will not lead us to do anything without the intent of helping us. It is our choice, however, to enter His kingdom or to desert Him, to choose the path of servanthood or selfishness. Christ was faithful to the vision He had accepted. May He become our vision as we journey to the eternal kingdom.

Prayer: I have come to this point on my spiritual journey of Lent. Have I been steadfast to You or have I turned aside from the course You would have had me take? Open my eyes that I may see the road I am on. If I have gone astray, guide me back to Your path. Help me to not give up but follow Your road of servanthood. I praise you, Lord, because You are my King. Amen.

Nailing Our Sins Upon the Cross

Symbol: a nail

Memory Verse: "He took this list of sins and destroyed it by nailing it to Christ's cross." Colossians 2:14 (TLB)

Songs to Sing:
  "It Is Well with My Soul"
  "Spirit of God, Descend Upon My Heart"
  "He Never Said a Mumbalin' Word"

Nailing Our Sins Upon the Cross
(CHILDREN)

Scriptures: Isaiah 53:5-6; Luke 24:33-40; John 20:24-29; Colossians 2:13-15

Devotion: Have you ever gotten a cut in your hand or foot? It hurts, doesn't it? After a while though, a scab forms over it to protect it from germs. It's kind of like God putting His bandage on the cut, so it will be healed. Did you know that Jesus was willing to be hurt for you, so you could be protected from bad things? He was taken to a hill and put on a cross. Nails were pounded into His hands and feet. This was a terrible thing to do to someone, but the cuts from the nails show us how much He loves you and me. He was willing to be punished for the bad things we do, but He had done nothing wrong. The nails in His hands and feet hurt Him very much, but when this happened, Jesus was forgiving us for all the bad things we have ever done. It was like He was covering our cut or sin with Himself, so that we could be healed.

There was another time Jesus showed us the nail marks in his hands. On the Sunday night after Jesus had died, the disciples were together in a room talking to each other. The door was locked, but suddenly, Jesus appeared before them! They couldn't believe their eyes! Jesus showed His friends the hurt places in His hands where the nails had been. By seeing the nail marks, the disciples remembered how Jesus had died for each one of them. Whenever we see a nail, let's remember how much Jesus loves us. And just like Jesus, let's also remember to forgive others when they do something bad to us.

Questions:
What did Jesus do wrong?
What are in Jesus' hands and feet?
Why did Jesus let the bad people kill Him?
Does Jesus love you?

Prayer: Lord Jesus, we cannot see You or Your nail marked hands, but we know You are our Living Savior. Thank You for letting our sins be nailed to the cross. Thank You for forgiving us and healing us. Help us to forgive others who hurt us. Amen.

A Lenten Activity: Have your children think of something bad they might have done or thought and write it on a piece of paper. Nail the paper to a cross. Remind them that Jesus has nailed their sins to the cross and remembers them no more, then take the child's paper from the cross and throw it away. Also, show a picture of the Passion Flower. Spanish missionaries discovered this beautiful flower in South America during the sixteenth century and used its parts to tell the story of Christ's crucifixion. The purple corona represents the crown of thorns, the central seed pod–the cross, the three stigma–the nails, and the five stamens–the five wounds.

Nailing Our Sins Upon the Cross
(ADULTS)

Scriptures: Isaiah 53:5-6; Luke 24:33-48; John 20:24-29; Colossians 2:6-15

Devotion: "Reach Out and Touch Someone" has become an old household phrase. Marketed by a phone company, its intentions were for people to pick up the phone and stay in contact with a family member or friend. So it was with Thomas, the practical disciple who needed the physical contact of an earthly king. Instead, at the cross, Thomas was left with no one to reach out to, no one to touch. All of his dreams became victim to doubt. He needed proof, physical proof in a miracle, for Thomas knew Christ had died. It was easy for him to believe in Good Friday because he realistically knew what had happened at the crucifixion. A single nail had been driven into Christ's feet and then into a small olivewood board to keep the feet together. The forearms had been nailed to the horizontal bar. Christ was dead. There was little hope that God could replace death with life. It wasn't sound thinking.

It is hard for us to believe in the Resurrection. Sin and death make more sense to us because we know we are guilty of sin, and we are aware of death every day. God, however, has crucified our old nature and replaced it with a new nature. The Old Testament law demanded payment for sins. Christ's death on the cross paid in full our debt. Our sins were swept away and forgiven by God, so now we may experience unbroken contact with Him and freedom from the penalty of sin.

Thomas needed proof, so Jesus extended his hands one more time, a week after His resurrection. We are not told if Thomas put his fingers in the nail scarred hands. We do know that seeing the imprints, he believed. May we reach out and touch, not to seek proof, but to hold the hand of the One who brings healing to a world without hope. When we do, the Presence we seek will become as real as anything we will ever know.

Looking back at the crucifixion story, we also see another nail being used. Pilate allowed the inscription "This Is the King of the Jews" to be nailed on Jesus' cross. Our logical reasoning cannot comprehend this, and yet the miracle of the truth of God had been written.

Prayer: Dying Redeemer, grant us assurance of Your presence now and faith in Your eternal goodness. We reach out in praise and thanksgiving for canceling our sin on the cross. As You forgave, help us to reach out to those from whom we are estranged with forgiveness. We know our healing will come when we love others as ourselves. Amen.

His Pierced Side

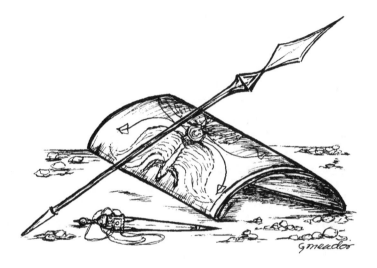

Symbol: a spear

Memory Verse: "God looks down from heaven on the sons of men to see if there are any who understand, any who seek God." Psalm 53:2 (NIV)

Songs to Sing:
  "Were You There"
  "Rock of Ages"
  "O Love Divine, What Hast Thou Done"

His Pierced Side
(CHILDREN)

Scriptures: John 19:31-37

Devotion: Do you remember how soldiers had nailed Jesus on the cross and left him there to die? As He was hanging and bleeding, they were playing a game on the ground underneath Him. They threw dice to see who would get His clothes. Jesus looked down on them and He was very hurt. He could have called the angels from heaven to destroy the mean people who were making fun of Him. Instead, He asked God to forgive them because they didn't know they were killing the only Son of God!

Before He died, Jesus hung on the cross for 6 hours. When the soldiers finished their game, one of them looked up at Jesus. He wanted to make sure Jesus was dead, so he took his spear that he used in fighting and made a big hole in Jesus' side. It was a hole big enough for someone to put his or her hand in. Blood and water came flowing out. Jesus was dead.

Jesus had paid for the sins of the world. He had not come with a spear in His hand to fight, but with love in His heart for you and me.

Questions:
Did the soldiers hurt Jesus?
Why did the soldier make a hole in Jesus' side?
Did Jesus die?

Prayer: Jesus, thank You for coming with love instead of a spear. We are so sorry You had to hurt on the cross. Forgive us when we don't realize we hurt You. Amen.

A Lenten Activity: Many things in nature remind us of Christ's sacrifice for us, and the sand dollar is one of these. Show the four small holes in the shell, which by legend represent the four nail holes in Christ's hands and feet. A larger hole represents the spear hole in Christ's side, and on one side there is a design which looks like the Easter lily. The star in the lily's center represents the star that appeared to the shepherds to lead them to Baby Jesus.

Break the sand dollar open, and you will find five white doves, symbolizing goodwill and peace.

His Pierced Side
(ADULTS)

Scriptures: Psalm 22:1, 14-18, 53:2-3, 69:20; Zechariah 12:10, 13:6-7; John 15:24-25, 19:34, 20:19-29; I John 5:1-12; Revelation 1:7

Devotion: Experiencing the death of a loved one can pierce someone to the very inner soul of emotion. In brokenness, the person tries to put the pieces back together, knowing that life continues, but with a very important part of that life gone forever. And yet, one does not wish for less pain because that would mean they would have loved less. Their love is seen through the pain of their broken heart.

Jesus bore the reproach and shame of the world on the cross. Taking sin upon Himself, He became separated from the One He loved the most, His Father. The cry, "My God, My God, why hast Thou forsaken me," shows the ultimate torture of His spiritual alienation from God. And yet, He readily accepted the agony of rejection from God and man to bring us life everlasting. How amazing is His love for us!

Surrounding the heart is a sac called the pericardium, containing a water-like substance. When the heart ruptures from congestive heart failure, blood often rushes into the pericardium. One theory of how Jesus died is that as the full weight of His body hung from the cross, breathing became almost impossible. The short and labored breathing caused stress-induced arrhythmia resulting in congestive heart failure. When pierced by the spear of the Roman soldier, the sac, fully extended, instantly released its contents. Hence the stream of water mixed with clotted blood came gushing forth from His blessed side showing the external evidence of the real cause of his death. Jesus died of a broken heart.

The disciple, John, witnessed Jesus' death with his own eyes, and he never forgot the horror of it. In the book of Revelation, John tells us that "those who have pierced Him shall see Him." While that means those who crucified Him at Golgotha, it also means many others who have pierced Christ with their insults, actions, and jealous motives. Have we pierced the One who loves us unconditionally? Have we broken His heart with our hate, our pride, and our selfishness?

Prayer: Lord, no greater love is this than that You laid down Your life for us. We humbly fall on our knees, seeking Your forgiveness for the times we have pierced You with our disobedience. Pierce our heart when we stray and bring us back to Your Love. Amen.

DAY THIRTY-SEVEN

A Servant Leader

Symbol: a washbasin and towel

Memory Verse: "A new command I give you: Love one another. As I have loved you, so you must love one another." John 13:34 (NIV)

Songs to Sing:
   "Freely, Freely"
   "Take My Life, and Let It Be"
   "This Little Light of Mine"

A Servant Leader

(CHILDREN)

Scriptures: Matthew 18:1-4; John 13:1-17; I John 4:20-21

Devotion: Have you ever tried to be first when you were playing a game? You didn't want anyone to be ahead of you, and you wanted to win. Maybe you were thinking about yourself instead of your friends. Jesus says we must love others just as much as we love ourselves. He told this to His disciples, too.

One day, His disciples asked Jesus who would be the greatest in heaven. Jesus brought a little child to them and told them if they wanted to be great, they needed to be like the child. What do you think that meant? The child was not big or strong. He didn't have a lot of money or a big job like his parents. But there was one thing he did have, and that was humility. Do you know what that is? Humility is when you put others first instead of yourself. That is the way to be great in Jesus' kingdom.

Jesus wanted to do something to show His disciples how not to be selfish. While He was eating His last supper with them, He thought of a way. The disciples' feet were dirty from walking and needed to be washed. Jesus stood up and did an amazing thing. He wrapped a towel around his waist, poured water into a basin, and began to wash the disciples' feet. They were so surprised and felt so bad that Jesus would be acting like a servant to them. But Jesus told them they needed to let Him do this. He washed the feet of all His disciples, and when He had finished, He sat down to talk to them.

Jesus told them that if they really loved Him, they would love others too. They would serve others by putting them first. He wants us to so the same thing, and if we do, we will have joy. Just remember JOY: Jesus first, Others second, and You last. If we do this, Jesus will be very happy too!

Questions:
How did Jesus show His disciples He loved them?
How can we show love for others?
What does the word *JOY* remind us of?

Prayer: Dear Jesus, thank You for loving us and showing us how to serve others. Help us to not be selfish because selfishness makes You sad. Help us think of ways we can serve others to make them happy. Then You will have JOY, and we will too. Amen.

A Servant Leader
(ADULTS)

Scriptures: John 13-17; Philippians 2:5-7; Acts 1:7; II Corinthians 1:3-7; Philippians 3:7-11

Devotion: Jesus was at the end of His leadership on earth. He knew God had put all things under His power. He had come from God and was returning to God. He also knew it would be hard for His disciples after He was gone. They would be like sheep without a shepherd, a team without their leader. And so, Jesus gathered His own in an upper room to give His last instructions to them. Over and over, He commanded them to love one another as He had loved them. Then Jesus did something that seemed very inappropriate and yet full of meaning. He girded a towel around his waist, took a basin of water, and began to wash His disciples' feet. By this example, He was giving a new and "uncomfortable" definition to leadership: true greatness is measured by serving.

It seems inconceivable that today's "what's in it for me" attitude be replaced by seeking opportunities to help others. Most people are more worried about who sits at the head table instead of who stoops to use the towel and washbasin. Doing good deeds or donating money is more important than knowing who is being served.

As a leader, Christ served others with a humbleness of heart. Leaders know the goal to be achieved and teach, correct, and encourage those of the same goal. Christ continuously taught the message of the gospel to His followers, and though He reproved His disciples often, He never ceased to love them and to take care of them. Leaders empower others to work for completion of the goal. Christ did not only want His disciples to be nice to each other, but He wanted to instill in them the power to fulfill God's mission. Leaders are active listeners. Christ was always patient and sympathetic, knowing that annoying interruptions were but opportunities to serve. Leaders are faithful. Those whom Christ loved, He loved them to the end. In the same way, we are called to be leaders.

There are blessings that come from serving. First, we gain empathy for others and become less prone to judge. Second, we become partners with Christ, sharing in His sufferings. Finally, we are privileged to fulfill God's mission of bringing others to the Greatest Servant of all.

We have been placed on a team. It could be in a family, a volunteer group, or a job. Wherever we are, Christ is calling us to kneel with Him at the feet of others, get our towels dirty, and become servant leaders.

Prayer: Lord, wash our feet and make us whole. Empower us with Your Holy Spirit to be servant leaders to the world. Amen.

The Last Supper

Symbol: the bread and cup

Memory Verses: "Do this in remembrance of me." Luke 22:19 (NIV)

"Whenever you eat this bread and drink this cup, you proclaim the Lord's death until he comes." I Corinthians 11:26 (NIV)

Songs to Sing:
  "Let Us Break Bread Together"
  "One Bread, One Body"
  "In Remembrance"

The Last Supper
(CHILDREN)

Scriptures: Luke 22:7-23

Devotion: Jesus and His friends had gathered to eat the Passover meal. The disciples didn't know it, but this would be their last supper together. Jesus knew He was going to die. He loved His disciples very much and didn't want them to be sad. He wanted to help them understand what was going to happen to Him. So, while they were sitting around the table, Jesus took some bread, gave thanks, and broke it. He gave each of the disciples a piece. He told them to eat some of the bread because it was His body. The disciples ate the bread, but they didn't understand what He meant. Then Jesus took a cup of wine and told His disciples to drink it. He told them it was His blood, which was poured out for them. The disciples drank from the cup, but they still did not understand what He meant.

He then told them that He was going away. He wanted them to get together often to eat the supper of bread and wine. This would be a way of remembering Him until He would come back again for all who loved Him. The very next day, Jesus died on the cross. In the Lord's Supper, He had shown His disciples that He was going to give His body and His blood for them. When Jesus arose from the grave, the disciples finally understood about the bread and the wine. They knew He had died for them.

Today, when we give our hearts to Jesus and love Him, we may celebrate the Lord's Supper. It is a celebration because we are remembering that Christ died and freed us from our sins. We are also showing others that we believe in Jesus and belong to Him. Taking the Supper will bring us closer to Jesus and to others who love Him.

Questions:
  What did Jesus give His disciples at their last meal
    together?
  What does He want us to remember?
  Who can celebrate the Lord's Supper?

Prayer: Jesus, we thank You for giving Yourself so that we might have life. Every time we come to Your table and take Your bread and wine, we will remember that You died for us because You loved us so much. We look forward to Your coming again when we may sit with You and fellowship with You forever. Amen.

A Lenten Activity: Share in the Lord's Supper with Your family or church. Also, hang a picture of Jesus in your child's room. Every time they look at it, they are to "remember" what Jesus did for them.

The Last Supper
(ADULTS)

Scriptures: Luke 22:7-23, 24:13-25; I Corinthians 11:17-34, 13:12

Devotion: The master had been commissioned for a great work. With tireless devotion, he dedicated himself to the fulfillment of it. His objective was to reveal man and the intention of the soul. For this purpose, he chose twelve ordinary men from the streets of the city. In this great work, mankind would not only see betrayal but also outstretched hands of offering and submissiveness to a Divine Will. After three years of labor, the master's hour had finally come.

Leonardo Da Vinci painted one of the most famous paintings ever, *The Last Supper*. Soon after completion in 1497, the painting, seen on the wall of an eating hall, began to disintegrate. By 1556, the painting had become only a muddle of blots. During the 17th century, a door was cut on the painting's wall because no longer was the painting considered worth saving. Yet, someone remembered. Clouded with years of flooding and inept restorations, the painting was given up for lost countless times. The final deathblow seemed to be during World War II when a bomb demolished the roof, exposing the painting to the elements for three years. Only a few isolated streaks of fading color were left. Still, someone remembered. Beneath the countless applications of colors, Leonardo's "outline" of his masterpiece remained, and with the meticulous restoration in 1999, the original colors and details were now revealed for centuries to come. All because someone remembered.

As Christians gather around the table to partake in the holy institution of the Lord's Supper, we are asked to remember. Remember God's divine outline of salvation for us. Remember Christ's willingness in coming to this earth to minister to us. Remember our betrayals and His amazing grace that forgives us of our sinfulness. Remember the bread and wine as metaphors of the work of Christ on the cross. Remember that in the giving of His life, Christ gave us life. Remember His Resurrection and the promise of His coming again. Remember we, as believers, have become the body of Christ, His Church. Remember that if this Holy Communion becomes a ritual or habit, it will lose its significance forever. May we cling to the meal of bread and wine, lest we forget His amazing grace and love toward us.

Prayer: God of mercy, we thank You for Your Great Plan of Salvation. May we celebrate Holy Communion by remembering our deliverance from sin by the death of Your Son. We confess our resentful attitude to others, for we are all sinners unworthy to sit at Your table. Yet, we are sinners saved by Your grace. In Your giving, we have received life. Thank You. Amen.

The Cross

Symbol: a cross

Memory Verse: "All we like sheep have gone astray; we have turned every one to his own way; and the LORD hath laid on him the iniquity of us all." Isaiah 53:6 (KJV)

Songs to Sing:
   "The Old Rugged Cross"
   "In the Cross of Christ I Glory"
   "At the Cross"

The Cross
(CHILDREN)

Scriptures: Isaiah 53:6; John 19:18-34

Devotion: Today is Good Friday. It is a very sad day because this was the day Jesus died. Jesus was always doing good and had never done anything wrong, but there were people who hated Him. The soldiers placed a heavy wooden beam on Jesus' back and made Him drag the cross through the streets. Jesus was very weak from the beatings the soldiers had given Him, so they forced a man named Simon to carry the cross the rest of the way to a hill outside the city. The whole time people were laughing and saying ugly things to Him. But His friends followed crying because they did not understand why He had to die. When they got to a hill called "The Skull," they pounded nails in His hands and feet and left Him to hang on the cross for hours between two thieves.

Jesus' mother was there with some of His followers, watching her son die. Jesus asked His friend John to take care of her. At noon, the sky turned black for three hours and everything was very dark. Then Jesus cried, "It is finished." He bowed His head and died. Jesus had finished what God wanted Him to do. This was a very sad day, but why do you think we call it Good Friday? It was good because Jesus died so you and I could have all our sins forgiven, and we could go to heaven to be with Him forever!

Questions:
What happened on Good Friday?
Who was there?
Why did Jesus die?

Prayer: Jesus, we can never thank You enough for what You did for us on the cross. We love You very much. Help us to show our love to You by living for You. Amen.

A Lenten Activity: Look at a dogwood blossom. The blossom is in the form of a cross, two long and short petals. In the center of the outer edge of each petal is a brown-tinged indentation stained with red, like a nail hole. The center of the blossom resembles a crown of thorns.

The Cross
(ADULTS)

Scriptures: Psalm 35:14-21, 22:1-18; Isaiah 52:13-15, 53; John 19

Devotion: Upon His bleeding back, the cross is laid. Taunted and spit upon like a criminal, He struggles along the path of sorrows until He falls beneath His load, exhausted. Simon of Cyrene relieves Him of His physical burden, but the heaviness of the sins of the world still lay upon Him. He is dragged to Calvary where nails are driven through His hands and feet. Every bone is wrenched out of place as the cross is lifted up between heaven and earth and falls with a thud into the deepness of the ground. A sign is placed above Him, ironically proclaiming "This Is The King of the Jews." Casting lots for His clothes, the soldiers offer Him some of their cheap wine to drink. People continue to hurl abuses at Him, wagging their heads in mockery. He retaliates with words of forgiveness. The taunting continues. Amidst all of this, Jesus turns His attention to the one on earth who loved Him most of all, His mother. He tenderly entrusts her keeping to John, His closest of friends. With a final cry, "It is finished," Jesus dies as the lambs are being slain for the Passover.

The Jews, too sensitive to touch a corpse on the Sabbath, are more concerned about removing His body before sundown. It was the customary practice to accelerate death by the breaking of the criminal's legs, forcing asphyxiation to occur. One look at the face with the matted beard stained with blood, sweat, and tears, tells a soldier he does not have to waste his time with this process. Jesus is already dead. Instead, the soldier plunges a spear into the side of Christ, resulting in a fountain of blood and water to gush forth. As in the sacrificial lambs, no bone is broken.

In the days when Christ was crucified, the cross was a punishment for criminals. Since Christ's death, the cross has become the symbol of atonement and self-denial for mankind. Jesus, the Lamb of God, is the Perfect and Final Sacrifice for the sins of the world. His sacrifice struck the deathblow to the devil's rule and the sacrificial system and established His eternal authority over the earth forever.

Prayer: Jesus, in You, we have found our rest. Help us take up Your Cross, renouncing our own needs and desires. By Your death, may we live to bring others to You, the Author and Finisher of our faith. Amen.

DAY FORTY

Waiting Time: The Body Wrapped in Linen

Symbol: cocoon with a butterfly emerging

Memory Verses: "While we look not at the things which are seen, but at the things which are not seen: for the things which are seen are temporal; but the things which are not seen are eternal." II Corinthians 4:18 (KJV)

"Blessed are they that have not seen, and yet have believed." John 20:29 (KJV)

Hymns to Sing:
   "Beneath the Cross of Jesus"
   "What Wondrous Love Is This"
   "Open My Eyes"

Waiting Time: The Body Wrapped in Linen
(CHILDREN)

Scriptures: Matthew 17:22-23; Mark15:43-47; Luke 23:50-56; John 20:29; Hebrews 11:1

Devotion: Jesus is dead. He died on the cross. It was a cruel death, and many people had been mean to Jesus. There is one good man, however, who had not been mean. His name is Joseph, and he has taken the body, wrapped white linen cloths around it, and put it into a tomb, which is a great hole in a rock.

Some women who watched Jesus die on the cross have come to the place where His body is laid. They watch the Roman guards roll a big stone in front of the hole. They are very sad because they think they will never see Him again. This was their Lord, their very best Friend. They have forgotten that Jesus had told them He would come back to life! Do you ever forget the good things Jesus promises you? Do you only believe in the things you see?

Inside the tomb, Jesus' body looks like it is dead, but something is going on inside the white cloths. Jesus' body is changing into a new body, and this body is even better. Before, Jesus had a body just like yours and mine, but now this new body can walk through doors and travel many miles very fast. This is the body that will live forever with God in heaven!

Let's think about a caterpillar. It looks like an ugly old worm, doesn't it? At a certain time, however, it begins to spin white silky threads around it to cover its body up—just like the body wrapped in white cloth. There is a waiting time, and it looks as if nothing is going on, but one day the thread covering or cocoon opens up, and do you know what comes out? A beautiful butterfly that can fly anywhere it wants to!

The women are waiting. They have no hope. But we

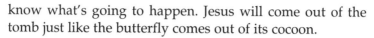

know what's going to happen. Jesus will come out of the tomb just like the butterfly comes out of its cocoon.

Questions:

What did Joseph do with Jesus' body?
Will His body stay in the tomb?

Prayer: Father, in Heaven, we are waiting for Easter. We thank Thee for Thy Word that tells us about what is going to happen. Help us not to forget the past and how Your Son, Jesus, died on the cross for us, so that our sins could be forgiven. Change us into beautiful new creatures who love You with all our hearts! Amen.

A Lenten Activity: Make Easter cookies (see Appendix). Your child will learn a tasty and important lesson.

Waiting Time: The Body Wrapped in Linen
(ADULTS)

Scriptures: Psalm 16:9-11; Matthew 17:22-23; Mark 15:42-47; II Corinthians 4; Hebrews 11:1

Devotion: Have you ever had times when you felt numb to the core? A failed relationship, job, or task left you empty and helpless. It seemed there was nothing to do but sink into depression and helplessness. You had no more to give, your spiritual vitality was zero, and you felt as if God didn't care.

Discouragement also abounded for the believers. Not only had their political deliverance been taken from them, they had also buried a dear friend. Certainly a deadness of spirit enveloped them as they saw His dead body being put in the tomb. Jesus had predicted His death but more important, He had told of His resurrection. Unfortunately, the disciples had heard only the first part of His words and forgotten the rest. All they saw was that it would take a miracle, an act of God, to change the circumstances. The Saturday between Good Friday and Easter was cold, silent, empty, and frightening.

God places waiting times in our lives to help us understand how He works. The gospel narrative of this Saturday is intent on helping us understand the mystery of the incarnation—that God had come among us in human form in order to suffer and die. The "Hallelujah" that would be proclaimed the next day would make no sense unless mankind knew that Jesus had fully died. The tomb, however, was not the end but the beginning of new life.

The life cycle of the butterfly is symbolic for the gospel message: First, there is the caterpillar, which stands for human life; next, the chrysalis, signifying death; and finally, the butterfly, emerging from the cocoon, portraying resurrection.

It's easy to lose heart and quit, but we can feel joy in spite of our deepest troubles. We may think we are at the end of our rope, but we are never at the end of hope. All our risks, humiliations, and trials are opportunities for Christ to demonstrate His presence and power working within us. We can have peace, not because of what we see, but because of what God has promised us. He did not abandon Christ to the grave nor will He abandon us.

Prayer: God, You have put a waiting period in my life. Help me to remember Your words of hope, and make them mine. Take me away from the busyness of this season to linger in the mystery of Your death, and prepare me for Your work. Teach me to take time out, and renew a right spirit within me. "Silently now I wait for Thee, ready my God, Thy Will to see. Open my eyes, illumine me, Spirit Divine."

The Empty Tomb

Symbol: an empty Easter egg

Memory Verse: "He is not here, for he is risen, as he said."
Matthew 28:6 (KJV)

Songs to Sing:
  "He Is Lord"
  "Christ the Lord Is Risen Today"
  "He Lives"

Easter
The Empty Tomb
(CHILDREN)

Scriptures: Matthew 28:1-6; I Corinthians 15:4; Revelation 1:18

Devotion: It is Sunday morning, and Jesus has been in the tomb for three days. Some women who are His friends have come to visit the tomb and to bring perfume for His body. They are very sad because Jesus has been so good to them, and they will never see Him again.

As they are coming to the tomb, they see someone sitting on a big stone. It is the stone that had closed the opening of where Jesus had been laid, but now it is rolled away! An angel, dressed in white, is sitting on it!

The women also see that the men who had guarded the tomb are lying on the ground as if they are dead! This frightens them, but the angel tells them to not be afraid. He tells them that Jesus isn't there but has come back to life! He tells them to look inside the tomb and see for themselves. When the women go inside, they see that it is just like an empty egg! Jesus is not there. He is alive! He is their Savior after all!

The stone had been rolled away so that everyone could see He was not in the grave anymore. The women remembered that Jesus had promised if anyone believes in Him, they will come back to life after they die. Just like a new life comes out of the egg, so will we go up to Heaven to live with Him forever! This made the women very happy. Are you glad that Jesus is alive?

Questions:
    What do the women see when they were coming to the
        tomb?
    What does the angel tell them?
    Why should we be happy that Jesus has risen?

Prayer: Jesus, we are so happy that You are alive. When You promise something, You will do it, and that makes us know we can trust you with our hearts. Thank You for coming to this earth and for dying for us. Thank you for coming back to life so that we can live forever with God. We love You and praise You, our Lord!

A Lenten Activity: Write messages such as "He is risen" on hard-boiled eggs with crayons before dyeing. The messages will miraculously appear on the dyed eggs! Also, have a special egg for the children to look for in an Easter egg hunt. When opened, instead of a surprise, the plastic egg will be empty, symbolizing that Christ is not in the tomb, but is alive, forevermore!

Easter
The Empty Tomb
(ADULTS)

Scriptures: Matthew 28:1-15; Mark 16:1-11; Luke 24:1-12; John 20:1-18; Romans 6:4; I Corinthians 15:4; Ephesians 2:5-6; Colossians 2:12-13; Revelation 1:18

Devotion: The symbol of the Easter egg is not found in the Bible, and yet it is the epitome of promised life. It is life sealed away for a time before new life literally bursts forth. The shell can be compared to a tomb in which a germ of life is held captive. When the shell is broken, this new life is free to enter into a new world.

An Egyptian legend tells how a bird, the phoenix, died in its own burning nest. It looked as if all were dead, but from an egg in the ashes, a new life came forth. Because of the similarity of Christ allowing Himself to die and the miracle of the Resurrection, the egg has become a Christian symbol of the Easter experience.

We have come to the end of our Lenten journey and have examined the truths of our faith. Jesus' resurrection is the key. We are delivered from our sinful past by Christ's death, and the power that brought Jesus back to life is available to us to bring our spiritually dead selves back to life. On this journey, we have examined our lives and realize that before we can walk in this newness of life, we must die to sin. We can't know the victory of the Resurrection without personally applying the Crucifixion. When we break the shells that hold us captive in sin and take hold of the hand of the Son of God, then we will experience the true power of everlasting life. We will understand and proclaim to the world, "He is not here. He is risen. He is living within my heart."

Prayer from "The Prayers of Peter Marshall:" We thank Thee for the beauty of this day, for the glorious message that all nature proclaims: the Easter lilies with their waxen throats eloquently singing the good news; the birds, so early this morning, impatient to begin their song; every flowering tree, shrub, and flaming bush, a living proclamation from Thee.

Open our hearts that we may hear it too! Lead us, we pray Thee, to the grave that is empty, into the garden of the Resurrection where we may meet our risen Lord. May we never again live as if Thou were dead!

In Thy presence restore our faith, our hope, our joy. Grant to our spirits refreshment, rest, and peace. Maintain within our hearts an unruffled calm, an unbroken serenity that no storms of life shall ever be able to take from us.

From this moment, O Living Christ, we ask Thee to go with us wherever we go; be our Companion in all that we do. And for this greatest of all gifts, we offer Thee our sacrifices of thanksgiving. Amen.

—Peter Marshall

Appendix

Lenten Activity Recipes

DAY TWO

JESUS IN THE WILDERNESS

Hot Cross Buns

3 cups flour
1 teaspoon salt
½ teaspoon allspice
½ teaspoon nutmeg
½ teaspoon cinnamon

¼ cup sugar
1 stick butter, melted
1 egg beaten
¾ cup currents or raisins
⅓ cup candied citron fruit

Yeast mixture:
1 tablespoon dry yeast
1 tablespoon sugar
⅔ cup warm milk

½ cup warm water
1 cup flour

Glaze:
2 tablespoons each: milk and water
3 tablespoons sugar

Begin by making the yeast mixture, mixing all ingredients and setting it aside to foam. In another bowl sift flour, salt, spices, and sugar. Add fruits and mix well. Combine butter and eggs and add to yeast mixture. Then add to flour mixture. Knead dough on floured surface, 8 to 10 minutes or until smooth and elastic. Add more flour if needed to keep dough from sticking.

Divide into 12 equal pieces and shape into round buns. Place buns far apart on greased baking sheet. Cover and let rise at warm room temperature for 45 minutes. Use a sharp knife to make an X or cross shape on surface of dough. Bake in a 425 degree oven for 15 or 20 minutes or until golden. Cool on rack. Make glaze by bringing ingredients to a boil in small saucepan for 2 minutes. Brush glaze over buns thickly.

DAY FOUR
GOD AMONG US

Cinnamon Rolls

1 pkg. Pillsbury Crescent
   Dinner Rolls
butter or margarine
granulated sugar

cinnamon
1 small pkg. crushed pecans
small plastic babies that
   are used in King Cakes

Unroll dough into 4 rectangles. Butter each rectangle gener-
ously. Sprinkle lots of sugar. Shake cinnamon to top. Add
pecans. Roll into small logs and put in refrigerator for 3
minutes. Take out and slice into ½ inch pinwheels. Place on
ungreased baking sheet, tucking ends under to prevent
unraveling. Bake at 350 degrees until done. Remove from
oven and glaze. Make powdered sugar glaze to spoon on
top while rolls are still warm. Place a plastic baby in each
roll and remind your child as they look inside, they will find
the Baby Jesus!

DAY SIX
THE PASSOVER LAMB

The Passover Seder (Supper)

Passover lasts seven or eight days and begins with a meal called Seder. This meal is made up of certain foods. Each has a special meaning.

Matzoth: wafers of unleavened bread. This is to remind us that the Israelites did not have time to wait for their bread to rise before leaving Egypt. For Christians, we should always be "ready to go" when Jesus returns.

Maror: bitter herbs, usually horseradish or onion. These herbs are a reminder of the bitter suffering in Egyptian slavery. As Christians, we remember the great cost of many who have suffered in sharing the good news of Jesus.

Haroseth: a mixture of chopped apples, nuts, cinnamon, and wine. This represents the mortar with which the Israelites were forced to make bricks for the Egyptians.

The shank bone of a lamb: This is a symbol of the lamb that was sacrificed for sins. To Christians, this represents Jesus, the perfect Lamb for the sins of all.

A roasted egg: a hard-boiled egg in the shell. Symbol of the free will offering that was given with the lamb. This is a gift of love. Jesus was God's ultimate gift.

Parsley or watercress and salt water: Parsley stays green year round and represents the continual rebirth. To Christians, this represents God's gift of everlasting life because of the Resurrection. Salt water represents the tears of sorrow.

Wine or grape juice: Wine represents joy. During the service, as each plague is mentioned, each person sips. A little showing joy being incomplete until total liberation. At the Last Supper, Jesus said the wine represented His own life's blood, poured out for us. He would have to die, so we could be free.

Elijah's cup: In the center of the table is a cup of wine that represents Elijah. The Israelites believed he would foretell the coming of the Messiah. Christians believe that John the Baptist was this "Elijah." For Christians, this cup is shared by everyone at the table in the joy that our hope has come true. Jesus is alive!

The father or grandfather is seated at the head of the table. The father passes the dishes to the family. As the meal progresses, the youngest son asks the father or grandfather the following question four different times: "Why is this night different from all other nights?"

The first time, the father answers as he serves the unleavened bread: "For on other nights we eat bread, but tonight we eat only matzoth." Then he explains the meaning of the bread.

The second time, the father answers as he serves the maror: "For on other nights we eat other vegetables, but tonight we eat only bitter herbs." He explains the meaning of the maror.

The third time, the father answers as he serves and explains the parsley, salt water, and haroseth: "For on other nights we do not dip our vegetables even once; but tonight, we dip twice." He dips the parsley into the salt water and reminds them of the tears and the sacrifice that was made. Next, he dips the haroseth, which sweetens the bitterness of the herb and reminds them that the sacrifice was sweetened by freedom.

The fourth time, the father responds, "For all other nights we eat sitting up, but tonight we all recline. Tonight, we celebrate our deliverance and freedom, so we sit in comfort and enjoy our freedom, wishing the same for all people."

For Christians as the meals ends, everyone shares the cup of joy symbolizing that Jesus became the final "Lamb" to be sacrificed in order that "our joy may be full."

DAY TEN
BREAD OF LIFE

Fresh Honey-Wheat Baked Bread

2 pkgs. dry yeast
½ cup warm water
1 egg
¾ cup honey
½ cup nonfat dry milk
1 tablespoon salt

2 tablespoons vegetable oil
1¾ cups warm water
3 cups whole wheat flour
4 to 4½ cups all-purpose
    flour

Dissolve yeast in ½ cup warm water in a large mixing bowl; let stand 5 minutes. Stir in egg and next 5 ingredients. Add whole wheat flour; beat at medium speed with an electric mixer. Stir in enough all-purpose flour to make a stiff dough.

Turn dough out onto a floured surface, and knead 5 minutes or until smooth and elastic. Cover and let rise in a warm place for 45 minutes.

Punch dough down; divide in half, and shape into two loaves. Place in well-greased 8 x 4 x 3 inch loaf pans; cover and let rise 30 minutes. Uncover and bake at 375 degrees for 30 minutes or until brown, shielding loaves with aluminum foil, if necessary, to prevent overbrowning. Remove bread from pans, and cool. Yield: 2 loaves.

DAY TWENTY-SEVEN
JESUS, THE MAN OF PRAYER

Pretzels

1½ cups warm water
1 package yeast
1 teaspoon salt
1 tablespoon sugar

4 cups flour
1 egg
Rock or table salt

Dissolve the yeast in warm water. Next add salt and sugar. Blend in flour. Knead dough until smooth. Cut into small pieces. Roll in ropes and twist into shape of praying hands. Place on lightly greased cookie sheets. Brush the pretzels with a beaten egg. Finally, sprinkle with salt. Bake at 425 degrees for 12 to 15 minutes.

DAY TWENTY-NINE
THE BETRAYER

The Jelly Bean Prayer

A bag full of jelly beans, colorful and sweet, is a prayer, is a promise, is a special treat!

> **RED** is for the blood He gave,
> **GREEN** is for the life He made.
> **YELLOW** is for the Sun so bright.
> **ORANGE** is for the edge of night.
> **BLACK** is for the sins we made.
> **WHITE** is for the grace He gave.
> **PURPLE** is for His hour of sorrow.
> **PINK** is for our new tomorrow.

DAY FORTY
WAITING TIME:
THE BODY WRAPPED IN LINEN

Easter Cookies

1 cup whole pecans	Zip-lock bag
1 teaspoon vinegar	Wooden spoon
3 egg whites	Tape
1 cup sugar	Bible
Pinch of salt	

Instructions to Live By: Preheat oven to 300 degrees. Place pecans in zipper baggie and let children beat them with the wooden spoon to break into small pieces. Explain that after Jesus was arrested, the Roman soldiers beat him. Read John 19:1-3.

Let each child smell the vinegar. Put 1 teaspoon vinegar into a mixing bowl. Explain that when Jesus was thirsty on the cross he was given vinegar to drink. Read John 19:28-30.

Add egg whites to the vinegar. Eggs represent life. Explain that Jesus gave His life to give us life. Read John 10:10-11.

Sprinkle a little salt into each child's hand. Let them taste it and brush the rest into the bowl. Explain that this represents the salty tears shed by Jesus' followers and the bitterness of our own sin. Read Luke 23:27.

So far, the ingredients are not very appetizing. Add 1 cup sugar. Explain that the sweetest part of the story is that Jesus died because He loves us. He wants us to know and belong to Him. Read Psalm 34:8 and John 3:16.

Beat with a mixer on high speed for 12 to 15 minutes until stiff peaks are formed. Explain that the color white represents the purity in God's eyes of those whose sins have been cleansed by Jesus. Read Isaiah 1:18 and John 3:1-3.

Fold in broken nuts. Drop by teaspoons onto wax paper covered cookie sheet. Explain that each mound represents the rocky tomb where Jesus' body was laid. Read Matthew 27:57-60.

Put the cookie sheet in the oven, close the door, and turn the oven off.

Give each child a piece of tape and seal the oven door. Explain that Jesus' tomb was sealed. Read Matthew 27:65-66.

Go to bed. Explain that they may feel sad to leave the cookies in the oven overnight. Jesus' followers were in despair when the tomb was sealed. Read John 16:20-22.

On Easter morning, open the oven and give everyone a cookie. Notice the cracked surface and take a bite. The cookies are hollow! On the first Easter, Jesus' followers were amazed to find the tomb open and empty. Read Matthew 28:1-9. Enjoy!

About the Author

Dean Meador Smith was born, raised, and educated in Hattiesburg, Mississippi. She graduated from the University of Southern Mississippi with a BMEd, a Bachelor's degree in Music Education and a Master of Arts in the Teaching of Language. She served in various positions such as Director of Adult, Children, and Youth Music and Puppet Ministries and Children and Youth Director for 24 years at Broad Street UMC and Heritage UMC. During this time she wrote several Christian musicals, plays, and curriculum programs for the church. She has also taught music and dance in the Hattiesburg and Forrest County Public schools.

Dean is currently teaching at the English Language Institute of the University of Southern Mississippi and enjoys leading creative teaching seminars for local and southeastern conferences of TESOL.

Dean is the author of the nationally published book, *The Advent Jesse Tree*, a book of Advent devotional books for children and adults. She is married to Eddie Smith and has three daughters, Elizabeth, Emily, and Erin.

About the Illustrator

Ginger Meador is a native of Hattiesburg, Mississippi. She graduated from the University of Southern Mississippi with a BS and MS in Education and Library Science. She taught in both public and private school systems in Mississippi until her retirement.

She experimented with art in different media from an early age. She preferred pen and ink drawing and realistic watercolor expression. She has illustrated two books, prior to *The Lenten Tree*, has exhibited her paintings, receiving awards for her work, and continues to work by commission.

The Meador family enjoys active involvement in The United Methodist Church. Ginger is grateful to God for each opportunity for service He provides in her life; however, she is especially thankful to be used as an artistic vessel for Him. See Ephesians 3:20-21.